R High Performance Programming

Overcome performance difficulties in R with a range
of exciting techniques and solutions

Aloysius Lim

William Tjhi

BIRMINGHAM - MUMBAI

R High Performance Programming

First published: January 2015

Production reference: 1230115

Published by Packt Publishing Ltd.
Livery Place
35 Livery Street
Birmingham B3 2PB, UK.

ISBN 978-1-78398-926-3

www.packtpub.com

Credits

Authors

Aloysius Lim

William Tjhi

Reviewers

Richard Cotton

Kirill Müller

John Silberholz

Commissioning Editor

Kunal Parikh

Acquisition Editor

Richard Brookes-Bland

Content Development Editor

Susmita Sabat

Technical Editor

Shiny Poojary

Copy Editor

Neha Vyas

Project Coordinator

Milton Dsouza

Proofreaders

Ameesha Green

Clyde Jenkins

Jonathan Todd

Indexer

Tejal Soni

Graphics

Sheetal Aute

Valentina D'silva

Production Coordinator

Komal Ramchandani

Cover Work

Komal Ramchandani

About the Authors

Aloysius Lim has a knack for translating complex data and models into easy-to-understand insights. As cofounder of About People, a data science and design consultancy, he loves solving problems and helping others to find practical solutions to business challenges using data. His breadth of experience—7 years in the government, education, and retail industries—equips him with unique perspectives to find creative solutions.

My deepest thanks go to God for the opportunity to write this book and share the knowledge that I have been given. My lovely wife, Bethany, has been a tremendous source of support and encouragement throughout this project. Thank you dear, for all your love. Many thanks to my partner William for his wonderful friendship. He has been a source of inspiration and insights throughout this journey.

William Tjhi is a data scientist with years of experience working in academia, government, and industry. He began his data science journey as a PhD candidate researching new algorithms to improve the robustness of high-dimensional data clustering. Upon receiving his doctorate, he moved from basic to applied research, solving problems among others in molecular biology and epidemiology using machine learning. He published some of his research in peer-reviewed journals and conferences. With the rise of Big Data, William left academia for industry, where he started practicing data science in both business and public sector settings. William is passionate about R and has been using it as his primary analysis tool since his research days. He was once part of Revolution Analytics, and there he contributed to make R more suitable for Big Data.

I would like to thank my coauthor, Aloysius. Your hard work, patience, and determination made this book possible.

About the Reviewers

Richard Cotton is a data scientist with a mixed background in proteomics, debt collection, and chemical health and safety, and he has worked extensively on tools to give nontechnical users access to statistical models. He is the author of the book *Learning R, O'Reilly*, and has created a number of popular R packages, including assertive, regex, pathological, and sig. He works for Weill Cornell Medical College in Qatar.

Kirill Müller holds a diploma in computer science and currently works as a research assistant at the Institute for Transport Planning and Systems of the Swiss Federal Institute of Technology (ETHZ) in Zurich. He is an avid R user and has contributed to several R packages.

John Silberholz is a fourth year PhD student at the MIT Operations Research Center, working under advisor Dimitris Bertsimas. His thesis research focuses on data-driven approaches to design novel chemotherapy regimens for advanced cancer and approaches to identify effective population screening strategies for cancer. His research interests also include analytical applications in the fields of bibliometrics and heuristic evaluation. John codeveloped *15.071x: The Analytics Edge*, a massive open online course (MOOC), which teaches machine learning and optimization using R and spreadsheet solvers.

Before coming to MIT, John completed his BS degree in mathematics and computer science from the University of Maryland. He completed internships as a software developer at Microsoft and Google, and he cofounded Enertaq, an electricity grid reliability start-up.

www.PacktPub.com

Support files, eBooks, discount offers, and more

For support files and downloads related to your book, please visit www.PacktPub.com.

Did you know that Packt offers eBook versions of every book published, with PDF and ePub files available? You can upgrade to the eBook version at www.PacktPub.com and as a print book customer, you are entitled to a discount on the eBook copy. Get in touch with us at service@packtpub.com for more details.

At www.PacktPub.com, you can also read a collection of free technical articles, sign up for a range of free newsletters and receive exclusive discounts and offers on Packt books and eBooks.

https://www2.packtpub.com/books/subscription/packtlib

Do you need instant solutions to your IT questions? PacktLib is Packt's online digital book library. Here, you can search, access, and read Packt's entire library of books.

Why subscribe?

- Fully searchable across every book published by Packt
- Copy and paste, print, and bookmark content
- On demand and accessible via a web browser

Free access for Packt account holders

If you have an account with Packt at www.PacktPub.com, you can use this to access PacktLib today and view 9 entirely free books. Simply use your login credentials for immediate access.

Table of Contents

Preface

In a world where data is becoming increasingly important, business people and scientists need tools to analyze and process large volumes of data efficiently. R is one of the tools that have become increasingly popular in recent years for data processing, statistical analysis, and data science. While R has its roots in academia, it is now used by organizations across a wide range of industries and geographical areas.

But the design of R imposes some inherent limits on the size of the data and the complexity of computations that it can manage efficiently. This can be a huge obstacle for R users who need to process the ever-growing volume of data in their organizations.

This book, *R High Performance Programming*, will help you understand the situations that often pose performance difficulties in R, such as memory and computational limits. It will also show you a range of techniques to overcome these performance limits. You can choose to use these techniques alone, or in various combinations that best fit your needs and your computing environment.

This book is designed to be a practical guide on how to improve the performance of R programs, with just enough explanation of why, so that you understand the reasoning behind each solution. As such, we will provide code examples for every technique that we cover in this book, along with performance profiling results that we generated on our machines to demonstrate the performance improvements. We encourage you to follow along by entering and running the code in your own environment to see the performance improvements for yourself.

If you would like to understand how R is designed and why it has performance limitations, the R Internals documentation (`http://cran.r-project.org/doc/manuals/r-release/R-ints.html`) will provide helpful clues.

This book is written based on open source R because it is the most widely used version of R and is freely available to anybody. If you are using a commercial version of R, check with your software vendor to see what performance improvements they might have made available to you.

The R community has created many new packages to improve the performance of R, which are available on the Comprehensive R Archive Network (CRAN) (http://cran.r-project.org/). We cannot analyze every package on CRAN—there are thousands of them—to see if they provide performance enhancements for specific operations. Instead, this book focuses on the most common tasks for R programmers and introduces techniques that you can use on any R project.

What this book covers

Chapter 1, Understanding R's Performance – Why Are R Programs Sometimes Slow?, kicks off our journey by taking a peek under R's hood to explore the various ways in which R programs can hit performance limits. We will look at how R's design sometimes creates performance bottlenecks in R programs in terms of computation (CPU), memory (RAM), and disk input/output (I/O).

Chapter 2, Profiling – Measuring Code's Performance, introduces a few techniques that we will use throughout the book to measure the performance of R code, so that we can understand the nature of our performance problems.

Chapter 3, Simple Tweaks to Make R Run Faster, describes how to improve the computational speed of R code. These are basic techniques that you can use in any R program.

Chapter 4, Using Compiled Code for Greater Speed, explores the use of compiled code in another programming language such as C to maximize the performance of our computations. We will see how compiled code can perform faster than R, and look at how to integrate compiled code into our R programs.

Chapter 5, Using GPUs to Run R Even Faster, brings us to the realm of modern accelerators by leveraging Graphics Processing Units (GPUs) to run complex computations at high speed.

Chapter 6, Simple Tweaks to Use Less RAM, describes the basic techniques to manage and optimize RAM utilization of your R programs to allow you to process larger datasets.

Chapter 7, Processing Large Datasets with Limited RAM, explains how to process datasets that are larger than the available RAM using memory-efficient data structures and disk resident data formats.

Chapter 8, Multiplying Performance with Parallel Computing, introduces parallelism in R. We will explore how to run code in parallel in R on a single machine and on multiple machines. We will also look at the factors that need to be considered in the design of our parallel code.

Chapter 9, Offloading Data Processing to Database Systems, describes how certain computations can be offloaded to an external database system. This is useful to minimize Big Data movements in and out of the database, and especially when you already have access to a powerful database system with computational power and speed for you to leverage.

Chapter 10, R and Big Data, concludes the book by exploring the use of Big Data technologies to take R's performance to the limit.

If you are in a hurry, we recommend that you read the following chapters first, then supplement your reading with other chapters that are relevant for your situation:

*   *Chapter 1, Understanding R's Performance – Why Are R Programs Sometimes Slow?*
*   *Chapter 2, Profiling – Measuring Code's Performance*
*   *Chapter 3, Simple Tweaks to Make R Run Faster*
*   *Chapter 6, Simple Tweaks to Use Less RAM*

What you need for this book

All the codes in this book were developed in R 3.1.1 64-bit on Mac OS X 10.9. Wherever possible, they have also been tested on Ubuntu desktop 14.04 LTS and Windows 8.1. All code examples can be downloaded from `https://github.com/r-high-performance-programming/rhpp-2015`.

To follow along the code examples, we recommend you to install R 3.1.1 64-bit or a later version in your environment.

We also recommend you to run R in a Unix environment (this includes Linux and Mac OS X). While R runs on Windows, some packages that we will use, for example, "bigmemory" runs only in a Unix environment. Whenever there are differences between Unix and Windows in our code examples, we will indicate them.

You will need the 64-bit version of R, as certain operations (for example, creating a vector with 231 or more elements) are not possible in the 32-bit version. Also, the 64-bit version of R can make use of as much memory as is available on your system, whereas the 32-bit version is limited to not more than 4 GB of memory (on some operating systems, the limit can be as low as 2 GB).

You will also need to install packages in your R environment, as the examples in several chapters will depend on additional packages.

The examples in some chapters require other software or packages to run. These will be listed in the respective chapters along with installation instructions.

If you do not have access to some of the software and tools required for the examples, you can run them on Amazon Web Services (AWS). In particular, the examples in *Chapter 5, Using GPUs to Run R Even Faster*, require a computer with an NVIDIA GPU with CUDA capabilities; those in *Chapter 9, Offloading Data Processing to Database Systems*, require various database systems; and those in *Chapter 10, R and Big Data*, require Hadoop.

To use AWS, log in to http://aws.amazon.com/ with your Amazon account. Create an account if you do not have one. Creating an account is free, but there are charges for using servers, storage, and other resources. Consult the AWS website for the latest prices in your preferred region.

AWS services are provided in different regions around the world. At the time of writing this book, there are eight regions — three in the United States, one in Europe, three in the Asia Pacific, and one in South America. Pick any region you like, such as the one closest to where you are or the one with the lowest prices. To select a region, go to AWS Console (http://console.aws.amazon.com) and select the region in the upper-right corner. Once you have selected a region, use the same region for all the AWS resources you need for the examples in this book.

Before setting up any compute resource, such as a server or Hadoop cluster, you need a key pair to log in to the server. If you do not already have an AWS Elastic Compute Cloud (EC2) key pair, follow these steps to generate one:

1. Go to AWS Console and click on EC2.
2. Click on Key Pairs in the menu on the left.
3. Click on Create Key Pair.
4. Enter a name for the new key pair (for example, mykey).
5. Once you click on Create, the private key (for example, mykey.pem) will be downloaded on your computer.

On Linux and Mac OS X, change the permissions of the private key file to allow only the read access to the owner; this can be done with chmod 400 mykey.pem in a Terminal window.

Who this book is for

If you are already an R programmer and you want to find ways to improve the efficiency of your code, then this book is for you. While you need to be familiar with and comfortable using R, you do not need deep expertise in the language. The skills that you need to benefit from this book are:

- Installing, upgrading and running R on your computer
- Installing and upgrading CRAN packages within your R environment
- Creating and manipulating basic data structures like vectors, matrices, lists, and data frames
- Using and converting between different R data types
- Performing arithmetic, logical, and other basic R operations
- Using R control statements such as if, for, while, and repeat
- Writing R functions
- Plotting charts using R Graphics

If you are new to R and want to learn how to write R programs, there are many books, online courses, tutorials, and other resources available. Just search for them using your favorite search engine.

Conventions

In this book, you will find a number of styles of text that distinguish among different kinds of information. Here are some examples of these styles, and an explanation of their meaning.

Code words in text, database table names, folder names, filenames, file extensions, pathnames, dummy URLs, user input, and Twitter handles are shown as follows: "To compile the function, we will use the cmpfun() function in the compiler package."

A block of code is set as follows:

```
fibonacci_rec <- function(n) {
    if (n <= 1) {
        return(n)
    }
    return(fibonacci_rec(n - 1) + fibonacci_rec(n - 2))
}
```

New terms and **important words** are shown in bold. Words that you see on the screen, in menus or dialog boxes for example, appear in the text like this: "Be sure to select the **Package authoring installation** and **Edit the system PATH** options in the installation wizard."

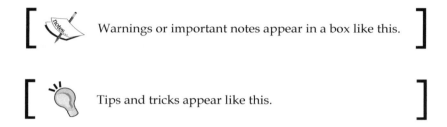

Warnings or important notes appear in a box like this.

Tips and tricks appear like this.

Reader feedback

Feedback from our readers is always welcome. Let us know what you think about this book—what you liked or may have disliked. Reader feedback is important for us to develop titles that you really get the most out of.

To send us general feedback, simply send an e-mail to feedback@packtpub.com, and mention the book title via the subject of your message.

If there is a topic that you have expertise in and you are interested in either writing or contributing to a book, see our author guide on www.packtpub.com/authors.

Customer support

Now that you are the proud owner of a Packt book, we have a number of things to help you to get the most from your purchase.

Downloading the example code

You can download the example code files for all Packt books you have purchased from your account at http://www.packtpub.com. If you purchased this book elsewhere, you can visit http://www.packtpub.com/support and register to have the files e-mailed directly to you.

Errata

Although we have taken every care to ensure the accuracy of our content, mistakes do happen. If you find a mistake in one of our books — maybe a mistake in the text or the code — we would be grateful if you would report this to us. By doing so, you can save other readers from frustration and help us improve subsequent versions of this book. If you find any errata, please report them by visiting http://www.packtpub.com/submit-errata, selecting your book, clicking on the **errata submission form** link, and entering the details of your errata. Once your errata are verified, your submission will be accepted and the errata will be uploaded on our website, or added to any list of existing errata, under the Errata section of that title. Any existing errata can be viewed by selecting your title from http://www.packtpub.com/support.

Piracy

Piracy of copyright material on the Internet is an ongoing problem across all media. At Packt, we take the protection of our copyright and licenses very seriously. If you come across any illegal copies of our works, in any form, on the Internet, please provide us with the location address or website name immediately so that we can pursue a remedy.

Please contact us at copyright@packtpub.com with a link to the suspected pirated material.

We appreciate your help in protecting our authors, and our ability to bring you valuable content.

Questions

You can contact us at questions@packtpub.com if you are having a problem with any aspect of the book, and we will do our best to address it.

1
Understanding R's Performance – Why Are R Programs Sometimes Slow?

R is a great tool used for statistical analysis and data processing. When it was first developed in 1993, it was designed as a tool that would teach data analysis courses. Because it is so easy to use, it became more and more popular over the next 20 years, not only in academia, but also in government and industry. R is also an open source tool, so its users can use it for free and contribute new statistical packages to the R public repository called the **Comprehensive R Archive Network (CRAN)**. As the CRAN library became richer with more than 6,000 well-documented and ready-to-use packages at the time of writing this book, the attractiveness of R increased even further. In these 20 years, the volume of data being created, transmitted, stored, and analyzed, by organizations and individuals alike, has also grown exponentially. R programmers who need to process and analyze the ever growing volume of data sometimes find that R's performance suffers under such heavy loads. Why does R sometimes not perform well, and how can we overcome its performance limitations? This book examines the factors behind R's performance and offers a variety of techniques to improve the performance of R programs, for example, optimizing memory usage, performing computations in parallel, or even tapping the computing power of external data processing systems.

Before we can find the solutions to R's performance problems, we need to understand what makes R perform poorly in certain situations. This chapter kicks off our exploration of the high-performance R programming by taking a peek under the hood to understand how R is designed, and how its design can limit the performance of R programs.

We will examine three main constraints faced by any computational task—CPU, RAM, and disk **input/output (I/O)**—and then look at how these play out specifically in R programs. By the end of this chapter, you will have some insights into the bottlenecks that your R programs could run into.

This chapter covers the following topics:

- Three constraints on computing performance—CPU, RAM, and disk I/O
- R is interpreted on the fly
- R is single-threaded
- R requires all data to be loaded into memory
- Algorithm design affects time and space complexity

Three constraints on computing performance – CPU, RAM, and disk I/O

First, let's see how R programs are executed in a computer. This is a very simplified version of what actually happens, but it suffices for us to understand the performance limitations of R. The following figure illustrates the steps required to execute an R program.

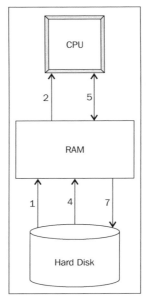

Steps to execute an R program

Take for example, this simple R program, which loads some data from a CSV file, computes the column sums, and writes the results into another CSV file:

```
data <- read.csv("mydata.csv")
totals <- colSums(data)
write.csv(totals, "totals.csv")
```

We use the numbering to understand the preceding diagram:

1. When we load and run an R program, the R code is first loaded into RAM.

2. The R interpreter then translates the R code into machine code and loads the machine code into the CPU.

3. The CPU executes the program.

4. The program loads the data to be processed from the hard disk into RAM (read.csv() in the example).

5. The data is loaded in small chunks into the CPU for processing.

6. The CPU processes the data one chunk at a time, and exchanges chunks of data with RAM until all the data has been processed (in the example, the CPU executes the instructions of the colSums() function to compute the column sums on the data set).

7. Sometimes, the processed data is stored back onto the hard drive (write.csv() in the example).

From this depiction of the computing process, we can see a few places where performance bottlenecks can occur:

*   The speed and performance of the CPU determines how quickly computing instructions, such as colSums() in the example, are executed. This includes the interpretation of the R code into the machine code and the actual execution of the machine code to process the data.

*   The size of RAM available on the computer limits the amount of data that can be processed at any given time. In this example, if the mydata.csv file contains more data than can be held in the RAM, the call to read.csv() will fail.

*   The speed at which the data can be read from or written to the hard disk (read.csv() and write.csv() in the example), that is, the speed of the disk input/output (I/O) affects how quickly the data can be loaded into the memory and stored back onto the hard disk.

Sometimes, you might encounter these limiting factors one at a time. For example, when a dataset is small enough to be quickly read from the disk and fully stored in the RAM, but the computations performed on it are complex, then only the CPU constraint is encountered. At other times, you might find them occurring together in various combinations. For example, when a dataset is very large, it takes a long time to load it from the disk, only one small chunk of it can be loaded at any given time into the memory, and it takes a long time to perform any computations on it. In either case, these are the symptoms of performance problems. In order to diagnose the problems and find solutions for them, we need to look at what is happening behind the scenes that might be causing these constraints to occur.

Let's now take a look at how R is designed and how it works, and see what the implications are for its performance.

R is interpreted on the fly

In computer science parlance, R is known as an interpreted language. This means that every time you execute an R program, the R interpreter interprets and executes the R code on the fly. The following figure illustrates what happens when you run any R code:

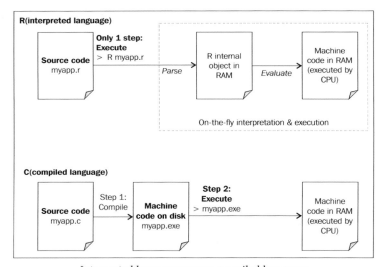

Interpreted language versus compiled language

R first parses your source code into an internal R object representation of all the statements and expressions in your R code. R then evaluates this internal R object to execute the code.

This is what makes R such a dynamic and interactive programming language. You can type R statements into the R console and get results immediately because the R interpreter parses and evaluates the code right away. The downside of this approach is that R code runs relatively slow because it is reinterpreted every time you run it, even when it has not changed.

Contrast this with a **compiled language** such as C or Fortran. When you work with a compiled language, you compile your source code into the machine code before you execute it. This makes compiled languages less interactive because the compilation step can take several minutes for large programs, even when you have made just a tiny change to the code. On the other hand, once the code has been compiled, it runs very quickly on the CPU since it is already in the computer's native language.

Due to R being an interpreted language, every time you run an R program, the CPU is busy doing two things: interpreting your code and executing the instructions contained in it. Therefore, the CPU's speed can limit the performance of R programs. We will learn how to overcome CPU limitations in chapters 3 to 5.

R is single-threaded

Another way in which R is CPU limited is that, by default, it runs only on a single thread on the CPU. It does not matter if you install R on a powerful server with 64 CPU cores, R will only use one of them. For example, finding the sum of a numeric vector is an operation that can be made to run in parallel in the CPU quite easily. If there are four CPU cores available, each core can be given roughly one quarter of the data to process. Each core computes the subtotal of the chunk of data it is given, and the four subtotals are then added up to find the total sum of the whole dataset. However in R, the sum() function runs serially, processing the entire dataset on one CPU core. In fact, many Big Data operations are of a similar nature to the summation example here, with the same task running independently on many subsets of data. In such a scenario, performing the operation sequentially would be an underuse of today's mostly parallel computing architectures. In *Chapter 8, Multiplying Performance with Parallel Computing*, we will learn how to write parallel programs in R to overcome this limitation.

R requires all data to be loaded into memory

All data that is processed in R has to be fully loaded into the RAM. This means that once the data has been loaded, all of it is available for processing by the CPU, which is great for performance. On the other hand, it also means that the maximum size of data that you can process depends on the amount of free RAM available on your system. Remember that not all the RAM on your computer is available to R. The operating system, background processes, and any other applications that are running in the CPU also compete for the RAM. What is available for R to use might be a fraction of the total RAM installed on the system.

On top of that, R also requires free RAM to store the results of its computations. Depending on what kinds of computations you are performing, you might need the available RAM to be twice or even more times as large as the size of your data.

32-bit versions of R are also limited by the amount of RAM they can access. Depending on the operating system, they might be limited to 2 GB to 4 GB of RAM even when there is actually more RAM available. Furthermore, due to memory address limits, data structures in 32-bit versions of R can contain at most $2^{31}-1$ = *2,147,483,647* elements. Because of these limits, you should use the 64-bit versions of R whenever you can.

 In all versions of R prior to 3.0, even 64-bit versions, vectors and other data structures faced this 2,147,483,647-element limit. If you have data that exceeds this size, you need to use a 64-bit version of R 3.0 or one of its later versions.

What happens when we try to load a dataset that is larger than the available RAM? Sometimes, the data loads successfully, but once the available RAM is used up, the operating system starts to swap the data in RAM into a swapfile on the hard disk. This is not a feature of R; it depends on the operating system. When this happens, R thinks that all the data has been loaded into the RAM when in fact the operating system is hard at work in the background swapping data between RAM and the swapfile on the disk. When such a situation occurs, we have a disk I/O bottleneck on top of the memory bottleneck. Because disk I/O is so slow (hard drive's speed is typically measured in milliseconds, while RAM's speed in nanoseconds), it can cause R to appear as if it is frozen or becomes unresponsive. Of the three performance limitations we looked at, disk I/O often has the largest impact on R's performance.

Chapter 6, Simple Tweaks to Use Less RAM and *Chapter 7, Processing Large Datasets with Limited RAM* will discuss how to optimize memory usage and work with datasets that are too large to fit into the memory.

Algorithm design affects time and space complexity

There is one other performance factor that we have not discussed—your code. The types of computations and algorithms that you run can have a huge impact on performance. Computer scientists describe the performance characteristics of programs in terms of complexity. In particular, we are concerned about two types of complexities:

- **Time complexity**: This refers to the computing time required to run an R program in relation to the size of the data being processed

- **Space complexity**: This refers to the memory that is required to run an R program in relation to the size of the data being processed

Let's look at an example of time complexity. Suppose that we need to write a function to compute the *nth* Fibonacci number, that is, a number in the sequence 0, 1, 1, 2, 3, 5, 8, 13, ... where each number is the sum of the previous two numbers. A simple way to do this would be to write a recursive function such as:

```
fibonacci_rec <- function(n) {
    if (n <= 1) {
        return(n)
    }
    return(fibonacci_rec(n - 1) + fibonacci_rec(n - 2))
}
```

Since the *nth* Fibonacci number is the sum of the *(n-1)th* and *(n-2)th* Fibonacci numbers, this function simply calls itself to compute the previous two numbers, then adds them up. Let's see how long it takes to compute the 25th Fibonacci number using the microbenchmark() function from the microbenchmark package, which can be downloaded and installed from CRAN (we will take a closer look at how to use this function in *Chapter 2, Measuring Code's Performance*):

```
microbenchmark(fibonacci_rec(25), unit = "ms")
## Unit: milliseconds
##                 expr      min     lq     mean   median       uq
##    fibonacci_rec(25) 170.1014  179.8 191.4213 183.5275 197.5833
##       max neval
##  253.1433   100
```

It took a median of 184 milliseconds. Because of the way the recursion works, there is a lot of unnecessary repetition. For example, to compute the 25th Fibonacci number, we need to compute the 23rd and 24th numbers in the sequence. But, computing the 24th number also involves computing the 23rd number, so the 23rd number is computed twice. And the 22nd number is needed to compute both the 23rd and 24th numbers, and so on.

We can reduce this repetition by computing each number only once. The following code presents an alternative implementation of the Fibonacci function that does just that. It computes the Fibonacci numbers in sequence from smallest to largest and remembers the numbers that it has computed in the numeric vector `fib`. Thus, each Fibonacci number is computed only once:

```
fibonacci_seq <- function(n) {
    if (n <= 1) {
        return(n)
    }
    # (n+1)th element of this vector is the nth Fibonacci number
    fib <- rep.int(NA_real_, n + 1)
    fib[1] <- 0
    fib[2] <- 1
    for (i in 2:n) {
        fib[i + 1] <- fib[i] + fib[i - 1]
    }
    return(fib[n + 1])
}
```

>
> **Downloading the example code**
> You can download the example code files for all Packt books you have purchased from your account at http://www.packtpub. com. If you purchased this book elsewhere, you can visit http://www.packtpub.com/support and register to have the files e-mailed directly to you.

By benchmarking this sequential function, we see that it takes a median of 0.04 milliseconds to run, a reduction of 99.98 percent from the recursive version!

```
microbenchmark(fibonacci_seq(25), unit = "ms")
## Unit: milliseconds
##                 expr     min       lq      mean    median       uq
##    fibonacci_seq(25) 0.03171 0.036133 0.0446416 0.0405555 0.04459
##                       max neval
##                  0.114714   100
```

To demonstrate the concept of time complexity, we ran the benchmark for different values of *n* ranging from 0 to 50. The median execution times are shown in the following figure:

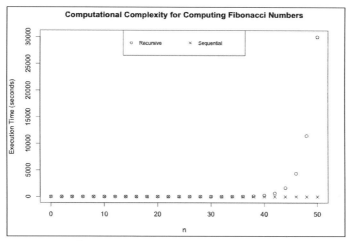

Execution time of recursive versus sequential versions of Fibonacci function

As we increase the value of *n*, the execution time of the recursive version of the Fibonacci function increases exponentially. It is roughly proportional to 1.6^n — every time *n* increases by 1, it gets multiplied by about 1.6 times. The execution time increased so fast that it took too long to compute the Fibonacci numbers after the 50th one. On the other hand, though it is imperceptible from the chart, the execution time of the sequential version increases linearly — every increase in *n* increases the execution time by 1.3 microseconds. Since the computational complexity of the sequential version is much lower than that of the recursive version, it will perform much better as *n* increases. As a case in point, with a modest value of *n=50*, the sequential version took a fraction of a millisecond to get computed while the recursive version took over eight hours!

Though we will not do it here, a similar exercise can be conducted in order to compare the space complexity of different algorithms. Given a certain amount of computational resources, your choice of algorithm and the design of your code can have a big impact on your R program's ability to achieve the desired level of performance.

Summary

In this chapter, we saw how R programs can sometimes encounter the three constraints faced by computing performance—CPU, RAM, and disk I/O. We looked into R's design and learned how its interpreted and single-threaded nature can cause it to run slowly, and how it can encounter memory and disk I/O limitations when data becomes too big to fit into the RAM. Finally, we looked at how the design of R code plays an important role in determining the performance using a comparison between two implementations of the Fibonacci function with very different performance characteristics.

These performance issues are not insurmountable. The rest of this book will show you different ways to overcome or work around them and unlock the hidden potential of R.

2
Profiling – Measuring Code's Performance

The first step to improve the performance of R programs is to identify where the performance bottlenecks are occurring. To do this, we **profile** or measure the performance of an R program as it runs with respect to various measures such as execution time, memory utilization, CPU utilization, and disk I/O. This gives us a good idea of how the program and its parts perform, so that we can tackle the biggest bottlenecks first. This chapter will show you how to use a few simple tools to measure the performance of R programs.

The 80/20 rule is applied here. 80 percent of the possible performance improvements can usually be achieved by tackling 20 percent of the largest performance problems. We will look at how to determine which problems to solve first in order to get maximum improvement in the least amount of time and effort.

This chapter covers the following topics:

- Measuring the total execution time
- Profiling the execution time
- Profiling the memory utilization
- Monitoring memory utilization, CPU utilization, and disk I/O using OS tools
- Identifying and resolving bottlenecks

Measuring total execution time

When people say that their program is not performing well, they are often referring to the **execution time** or the time it takes to complete the execution of the program. Execution time is probably the most important performance measure in many contexts as it is has a direct impact on people and processes. A shorter execution time means the R programmer can perform his or her analysis more quickly to derive insights faster.

It turns out that execution time is also the easiest performance characteristic that can be measured accurately and in detail (though not always the easiest to solve). Therefore, we will start learning about the way to profile an R code by learning to measure the execution time of R programs. We will learn three different tools to do this: `system.time()`, `benchmark()`, and `microbenchmark()`.

Measuring execution time with system.time()

The first profiling tool we will learn about is `system.time()`. It is a very useful tool that we can use to measure the execution time of any R expression.

Say we want to find out how long it takes to generate 100 million uniform random variables. Take a look at the following statement and the output when it is run in the R console:

```
system.time(runif(1e8))
##   user  system elapsed
## 2.969   0.166   3.138
```

The `runif(1e8)` expression generates 100 million random values between 0 and 1. In order to measure how long it takes to run this command, we simply pass this expression to `system.time()`.

The output contains three elements, all measured in seconds:

- **User time**: This element is the CPU time charged for the execution of user instructions of the given expression, for example, looping through an array. It does not include CPU time used by other processes (for example, if the computer happens to be running a virus scan in the background, the CPU time taken by it is not counted).

- **System time**: System time is the CPU time charged for the execution of system instructions on behalf of the given expression, for example, opening and closing files, or allocating and freeing memory. This does not include CPU time used by other processes.

- **Elapsed time**: Elapsed time is the total clock time taken to execute the given expression. It includes the time that the CPU has spent on other processes and time spent in waiting (for example, waiting for a file to be opened for reading). Sometimes, elapsed time is longer than the sum of user time and system time because the CPU is multitasking on other processes, or it has to wait for resources such as files and network connections to be available. At other times, elapsed time is shorter than the sum of user time and system time. This can happen when multiple threads or CPUs are used to execute the expression. For example, a task that takes 10 seconds of user time can be completed in 5 seconds if there are two CPUs sharing the load.

Most of the time, we are interested in the total elapsed time to execute the given expression. When the expression is executed on a single thread (the default for R), the elapsed time is usually very close to the sum of the user time and system time. If that is not the case, either the expression has spent time waiting for resources to be available, or there were many other processes on the system competing for the CPU's time.

It is best to shut down any unnecessary programs and processes on the system before running system.time() in order to reduce the competition for the CPU's time and to get an accurate measurement. Of course, the antivirus software or any other critical system software should not be turned off.

The system.time() declaration actually returns a vector with five elements but its print() function displays only the first three. To see all the five elements, we can call print(unclass(system.time(expr))). The other two elements are the system and user times for the execution of any child processes spawned by expr. On Windows machines, these are not available and will always be given as NA.

This is what happens when we run system.time() a few more times with the same expression:

```
system.time(runif(1e8))
##   user  system elapsed
## 2.963   0.160   3.128
system.time(runif(1e8))
##   user  system elapsed
## 2.971   0.162   3.136
system.time(runif(1e8))
##   user  system elapsed
## 2.944   0.161   3.106
```

By running `system.time()` repeatedly, we get slightly different results each time because R's overheads, OS caching mechanisms, other running processes, and many other factors might have a slight impact on the execution time.

Repeating time measurements with rbenchmark

It is sometimes helpful to run the same expression multiple times and get the average execution time, or even the distribution of execution times over multiple runs. The rbenchmark CRAN package lets us do this easily.

First, install and load the rbenchmark package:

```
install.packages("rbenchmark")
library(rbenchmark)
```

Next, use `benchmark()` to run the same random number generation task 10 times, by specifying `replications=10`:

```
bench1 <- benchmark(runif(1e8), replications=10)
bench1
##              test replications elapsed relative user.self
## 1 runif(1e+08)            10   32.38        1    29.781
##    sys.self user.child sys.child
## 1    2.565          0         0
```

The results show the total elapsed system and user time taken to generate 100 million uniform random variables over 10 repetitions. We can find the mean times taken per repetition using `within()` to divide the time measurements by the number of repetitions:

```
within(bench1, {
        elapsed.mean <- elapsed/replications
        user.self.mean <- user.self/replications
        sys.self.mean <- sys.self/replications
        })
##              test replications elapsed relative user.self
## 1 runif(1e+08)            10   32.38        1    29.781
##    sys.self user.child sys.child sys.self.mean user.self.mean
## 1    2.565          0         0        0.2565         2.9781
##    elapsed.mean
## 1       3.238
```

What if we want to know the execution times for each repetition, or the distribution of execution times over the repetitions? We can pass a vector instead of a single number as the replications parameter. For each element of this vector, benchmark() will execute the given expression the specified number of times. So we can get 10 samples of the execution of the random number generation once, as shown in the following code. In addition to the elapsed user and system time, benchmark() returns an additional column, relative, which indicates how each repetition's elapsed time is compared with the fastest one. For example, the first repetition took 1.011 times as long as the fastest repetition (the fourth one), or 1.1 percent longer to run:

```
benchmark(runif(1e8), replications=rep.int(1, 10))
##              test replications elapsed relative user.self
## 1   runif(1e+08)            1   3.162    1.011     2.971
## 2   runif(1e+08)            1   3.145    1.005     2.951
## 3   runif(1e+08)            1   3.141    1.004     2.949
## 4   runif(1e+08)            1   3.128    1.000     2.937
## 5   runif(1e+08)            1   3.261    1.043     3.021
## 6   runif(1e+08)            1   3.207    1.025     2.993
## 7   runif(1e+08)            1   3.274    1.047     3.035
## 8   runif(1e+08)            1   3.174    1.015     2.966
## 9   runif(1e+08)            1   3.172    1.014     2.970
## 10  runif(1e+08)            1   3.230    1.033     3.004
##     sys.self user.child sys.child
## 1      0.187          0         0
## 2      0.191          0         0
## 3      0.189          0         0
## 4      0.190          0         0
## 5      0.228          0         0
## 6      0.210          0         0
## 7      0.230          0         0
## 8      0.207          0         0
## 9      0.201          0         0
## 10     0.224          0         0
```

Measuring distribution of execution time with microbenchmark

The CRAN package microbenchmark provides yet another way to measure the execution time of an R expression. Though its microbenchmark() function only measures the elapsed time and not the user time or system time, it gives an idea of how the execution times across repeated runs are distributed. It also automatically corrects for the overheads related to the execution of the timing tests. The microbenchmark() function is very handy to measure short running tasks over many repetitions provided you do not need to measure the user or system times. We will use this tool many times throughout this book.

Install and load the microbenchmark package:

```
install.packages("microbenchmark")
library(microbenchmark)
```

Now, run the same random number generation task 10 times using microbenchmark():

```
microbenchmark(runif(1e8), times=10)
## Unit: seconds
##           expr      min       lq  median       uq      max
##    runif(1e+08) 3.170571 3.193331 3.25089 3.299966 3.314355
##    neval
##       10
```

The statistics shows the minimum, lower quartile, median, upper quartile, and maximum values of the elapsed time over 10 repetitions. This gives us an idea of the distribution of the elapsed times over different repetitions of the same expression.

Profiling the execution time

So far, we have seen how to measure the execution time of a whole R expression. What about a more complex expression with multiple parts such as calls to other functions? Is there a way to dig deeper and profile the execution time of each of the parts that make up the expression? R comes with the profiling tool Rprof() that allows us to do just that. Let's see how it works.

Profiling a function with Rprof()

In this example, we write the following `sampvar()` function to calculate the unbiased sample variance of a numeric vector. This is obviously not the best way to write this function (in fact R provides the `var()` function to do this), but it serves to illustrate how code profiling works:

```
# Compute sample variance of numeric vector x
sampvar <- function(x) {
    # Compute sum of vector x
    my.sum <- function(x) {
        sum <- 0
        for (i in x) {
            sum <- sum + i
        }
        sum
    }

    # Compute sum of squared variances of the elements of x from
    # the mean mu
    sq.var <- function(x, mu) {
        sum <- 0
        for (i in x) {
            sum <- sum + (i - mu) ^ 2
        }
        sum
    }

    mu <- my.sum(x) / length(x)
    sq <- sq.var(x, mu)
    sq / (length(x) - 1)
}
```

Within `sampvar()`, we define two utility functions:

- `my.sum()`: This computes the sum of a vector by looping over the elements of the vector.

- `sq.var()`: This computes the sum of the squared deviations of a vector from a given mean, by looping over the elements of the vector.

The `sampvar()` function first computes the sample mean, then the sum of squared deviations from that mean, and then the sample variance by dividing that sum by *n-1*.

We can profile the sampvar() function as follows:

```
x <- runif(1e7)
Rprof("Rprof.out")
y <- sampvar(x)
Rprof(NULL)
summaryRprof("Rprof.out")
## $by.self
##           self.time self.pct total.time total.pct
## "sq.var"      4.38    58.24       5.28     70.21
## "my.sum"      1.88    25.00       2.24     29.79
## "^"           0.46     6.12       0.46      6.12
## "+"           0.44     5.85       0.44      5.85
## "-"           0.28     3.72       0.28      3.72
## "("           0.08     1.06       0.08      1.06
##
## $by.total
##           total.time total.pct self.time self.pct
## "sampvar"       7.52    100.00      0.00     0.00
## "sq.var"        5.28     70.21      4.38    58.24
## "my.sum"        2.24     29.79      1.88    25.00
## "^"             0.46      6.12      0.46     6.12
## "+"             0.44      5.85      0.44     5.85
## "-"             0.28      3.72      0.28     3.72
## "("             0.08      1.06      0.08     1.06
##
## $sample.interval
## [1] 0.02
##
## $sampling.time
## [1] 7.52
```

This is how the code works:

1. The runif(1e7) expression generates a random sample of 10 million numbers.

2. The Rprof("Rprof.out") expression tells R to begin profiling. Rprof.out is the name of a file in which the profiling data is stored. It will be stored in R's current working directory unless another file path is specified.

3. The sampvar(x) expression calls the function we just created.

4. The `Rprof(NULL)` expression tells R to stop profiling. Otherwise, it will continue to profile other R statements that we run but do not intend to profile.

5. The `summaryRprof("Rprof.out")` expression prints the results of the profiling.

The profiling results

The results are broken down into a few measures:

- The `self.time` and `self.pct` columns represent the elapsed time for each function, excluding the elapsed time of other functions that are called by the function.

- The `total.time` and `total.pct` columns represent the total elapsed time for each function including the time spent inside function calls.

From the profiling data, we get some interesting observations:

- The `sampvar()` function's `self.time` is negligible (reported as zero), indicating that almost all the time taken to run `sampvar` is contributed by the functions that it calls.

- While `sampvar()` spent a total of 7.52 seconds, 5.28 seconds of this time was contributed by `sq.var()`, and 2.24 seconds by `my.sum()` (see `total.time` of `sq.var()` and `my.sum()`).

- The `sq.var()` function took the largest chunk of time (70.21 percent) to get executed and looks like a good place to start improving the performance.

- The R operators `-`, `+`, and `*` were extremely quick, taking not more than a total of 0.46 seconds each, even though they were executed millions of times.

`Rprof()` works by observing R's call stack as the R expression is running, and taking a snapshot of the call stack at fixed intervals (every 0.02 seconds by default) to see which function is currently executing. From these snapshots, `summaryRprof()` can compute how much time was spent in each function.

For a more intuitive view of the profiling data, we can use the `proftools` package. We will also need to install the `graph` and `Rgraphviz` packages from the Bioconductor repository:

```
install.packages("proftools")
source("http://bioconductor.org/biocLite.R")
biocLite(c("graph", "Rgraphviz"))
library(proftools)
p <- readProfileData(filename="Rprof.out")
plotProfileCallGraph(p, style=google.style, score="total")
```

The `plotProfileCallGraph()` function generates an intuitive visual plot of the profile data. We use the `google.style` template which shows functions with longer `self.time` in bigger boxes. We also specify `score="total"` to color the boxes according to `total.time`. The following figure shows the output of the same profiling data:

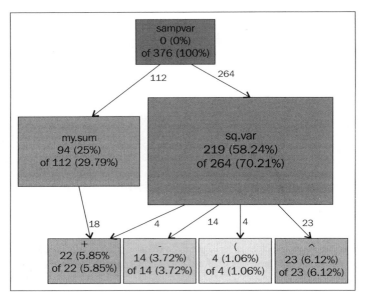

Profiling data for sampvar() rendered by plotProfileCallGrah()

We can see from `sampvar()` that it has the longest `total.time` of 100 percent. This is expected since it is the function that is being profiled. The next longest-running function is `sq.var()`, which accounts for 70.21 percent of the elapsed time. `sq.var()` also happens to have the longest `self.time`, which can be seen from the size of its box. Thus, `sq.var()` seems like a good candidate for the first step in addressing performance problems.

The `Rprof()` function is a useful tool to understand the performance of different parts of R programs and quickly spot bottlenecks that we can address to improve the overall performance of our R code.

Profiling memory utilization

Next, let's consider how to profile the memory utilization of R code.

One approach is to use `Rprof()` by setting the `memory.profiling` argument and the corresponding `memory` argument to `summaryRprof()`:

```
Rprof("Rprof-mem.out", memory.profiling=TRUE)
y <- sampvar(x)
Rprof(NULL)
summaryRprof("Rprof-mem.out", memory="both")
## $by.self
##            self.time self.pct total.time total.pct mem.total
## "sq.var"        4.16    54.88       5.40     71.24    1129.4
## "my.sum"        1.82    24.01       2.18     28.76     526.9
## "^"             0.56     7.39       0.56      7.39     171.0
## "+"             0.44     5.80       0.44      5.80     129.2
## "-"             0.40     5.28       0.40      5.28     140.2
## "("             0.20     2.64       0.20      2.64      49.7
##
## $by.total
##            total.time total.pct mem.total self.time self.pct
## "sampvar"        7.58    100.00    1656.2      0.00     0.00
## "sq.var"         5.40     71.24    1129.4      4.16    54.88
## "my.sum"         2.18     28.76     526.9      1.82    24.01
## "^"              0.56      7.39     171.0      0.56     7.39
## "+"              0.44      5.80     129.2      0.44     5.80
## "-"              0.40      5.28     140.2      0.40     5.28
## "("              0.20      2.64      49.7      0.20     2.64
##
## $sample.interval
## [1] 0.02
##
## $sampling.time
## [1] 7.58
```

The output now shows an additional column `mem.total` reporting the memory utilization of each function. For this example, it seems that it took 1,656 MB of memory to run `sampvar()`! This seems exceptionally high for computations on a numeric vector with 10 million elements, which would measure only 76.3 MB in the memory (you can check this by running `print(object.size(x), units="auto")`).

Unfortunately, `mem.total` is a misleading measure because `Rprof()` attributes the memory usage to the function that happens to be running when it takes a snapshot, but the memory could have been used by other functions and not have been released yet. Furthermore, R's garbage collector regularly releases unused memory to the operating system, so the actual memory being used at any given time might be vastly different from that reported by `Rprof()`. In other words, `Rprof()` gives an indication of the total amount of memory allocated while running an R code, but does not take into account the memory freed by the garbage collector.

To see how garbage collection affects memory utilization, we can run the following:

```
> gcinfo(TRUE)
y <- sampvar(x)
## Garbage collection 945 = 886+43+16 (level 0) ...
## 31.1 Mbytes of cons cells used (59%)
## 82.8 Mbytes of vectors used (66%)
## Garbage collection 946 = 887+43+16 (level 0) ...
## 31.1 Mbytes of cons cells used (59%)
## 82.8 Mbytes of vectors used (66%)
##... (truncated for brevity) ...
gcinfo(FALSE)
```

The `gcinfo(TRUE)` expression tells R to inform us every time the garbage collector releases memory. On our machine, the garbage collector was activated 272 times while running `sampvar()`! Although `Rprof()` reported that 1.7 GB of the memory was allocated in total, the garbage collector was hard at work to release unused memory so that R's total memory consumption stayed manageable at around 113.9 MB (*31.1 MB + 82.8 MB*).

Because `Rprof()` measures the cumulative allocated memory without accounting for garbage collection, it is not suited for determining whether an R program will exceed the available memory on a system. `gcinfo()` provides a clearer picture, albeit still an approximate one, by providing a snapshot of the memory consumption at every garbage collection interval.

The `gcinfo()` and `gc()` functions give pretty good estimates of memory utilization in this case because our code uses only standard R operations. Some R packages use custom memory allocators that `gcinfo()` and `gc()` are not able to track, so memory utilization can be underreported.

Monitoring memory utilization, CPU utilization, and disk I/O using OS tools

Unlike execution time, R does not provide any good tools to profile CPU utilization and disk I/O. Even the memory profiling tools in R might not provide a complete or accurate picture. This is where we turn to OS-provided system monitoring tools to keep an eye on the computational resources as we run R programs. They are task manager or resource monitor in Windows, activity monitor in Mac OS X, and `top` in Linux. When running these tools, look for the processes that represent R (usually called R or `rsession`).

The information that we get varies depending on the operating system, but here are the key measures of R's resource utilization to keep an eye on:

- **% CPU or CPU usage**: The percentage of the system's CPU time used by R

- **% memory, resident memory, or working set**: The percentage of the system's physical memory used by R

- **Swap size or page outs**: The size of memory used by R that is stored in the operating system's swapspace

- **Bytes read or written per second**: The rate of data being read or written from/to disk by R

In addition, we might also want to monitor these system-wide resource utilization measures:

- **% free memory**: The percentage of the system's physical memory that is available for use

- **Swap size or page outs**: The total size of memory that is stored in the OS's swapspace

The preceding measures are helpful in troubleshooting R's performance problems:

- **High CPU utilization**: A CPU is likely the main bottleneck of R's performance. Use the profiling techniques in this chapter to identify which parts of the code are taking most of the CPU's time.

- **Low CPU utilization, low free system memory with large swap size, and high disk I/O**: The system is likely running out of physical memory and is thus swapping memory onto the disk. Use the memory management techniques in *Chapters 6, Simple Tweaks to Use Less RAM*, and *Chapter 7, Processing Large Datasets with Limited RAM*, to reduce the memory required by the R program.

- **Sufficient free system memory with high disk I/O**: The program writes/ reads to disk very often. Check for any unnecessary I/O operations and store intermediate data in the memory if there is sufficient free memory.

Identifying and resolving bottlenecks

Now that we have covered the basic techniques to profile an R code, which performance bottlenecks should we try to solve first?

As a rule of thumb, we first try to improve the pieces of code that are causing the largest performance bottlenecks, whether in terms of execution time, memory utilization, or other measures. These can be identified with the profiling techniques covered earlier. Then we work our way down the list of the largest bottlenecks until the overall performance of the program is good enough.

As you can recall, the varsamp() example that we profiled using Rprof(). The function with the highest self.time was sq.var(). How can we make this function run faster? We can write it in the form of a vector operation my.sum((x - mu) ^ 2) rather than looping through each element of x. As we will see in the next chapter, converting loops to vectorized operations is a good way to speed up many R operations. In fact, we can even remove the function altogether since the new vector expression fits in one line:

```
# Compute sample variance of numeric vector x
sampvar <- function(x) {
    # Compute sum of vector x
    my.sum <- function(x) {
        sum <- 0
        for (i in x) {
            sum <- sum + i
        }
        sum
    }

    mu <- my.sum(x) / length(x)
    sq <- my.sum((x - mu) ^ 2)
    sq / (length(x) - 1)
}
```

```
x <- runif(1e7)
Rprof("Rprof-mem.out", memory.profiling=TRUE)
y <- sampvar(x)
Rprof(NULL)
summaryRprof("Rprof-mem.out", memory="both")
## $by.self
##           self.time self.pct total.time total.pct mem.total
## "my.sum"       3.92    85.22       4.60    100.00    1180.6
## "+"            0.66    14.35       0.66     14.35     104.2
## "-"            0.02     0.43       0.02      0.43      83.1
##
## $by.total
##           total.time total.pct mem.total self.time self.pct
## "my.sum"        4.60    100.00    1180.6      3.92    85.22
## "eval"          4.60    100.00    1180.6      0.00     0.00
## "sampvar"       4.60    100.00    1180.6      0.00     0.00
## "source"        4.60    100.00    1180.6      0.00     0.00
## "withVisible"   4.60    100.00    1180.6      0.00     0.00
## "+"             0.66     14.35     104.2      0.66    14.35
## "-"             0.02      0.43      83.1      0.02     0.43
##
## $sample.interval
## [1] 0.02
##
## $sampling.time
## [1] 4.6
```

This change shaved 2.98 seconds off the elapsed time and 477 MB off the total memory allocated while running the function.

Now the my.sum() function contributes to a significant 85 percent of the total elapsed time. Let's replace it with the sum() function from R, which runs much faster:

```
# Compute sample variance of numeric vector x
sampvar <- function(x) {
    mu <- sum(x) / length(x)
    sq <- sum((x - mu) ^ 2)
    sq / (length(x) - 1)
}
```

```
x <- runif(1e7)
Rprof("Rprof-mem.out", memory.profiling=TRUE)
y <- sampvar(x)
Rprof(NULL)
summaryRprof("Rprof-mem.out", memory="both")
## $by.self
##     self.time self.pct total.time total.pct mem.total
## "-"      0.08      100       0.08       100      76.2
##
## $by.total
##            total.time total.pct mem.total self.time self.pct
## "-"              0.08       100      76.2      0.08      100
## "sampvar"        0.08       100      76.2      0.00        0
##
## $sample.interval
## [1] 0.02
##
## $sampling.time
## [1] 0.08
```

Voila! In two simple steps, we reduced the elapsed time of sampvar() from 7.58 seconds to 0.08 seconds (a 99 percent reduction). Furthermore, the memory utilization as reported by Rprof() was also reduced from over 1.6 GB to a mere 76.2 MB (a 95.4 percent reduction). This reduction in memory allocation and garbage collection also played a significant part in speeding up our code.

Let's compare how fast our code runs compared to the R function var(), which is written in C for optimal performance (we will learn in *Chapter 4, Using Compiled Code for Greater Speed*):

```
library(microbenchmark)
microbenchmark(sampvar(x), var(x))
## Unit: milliseconds
##       expr      min       lq   median       uq      max neval
##  sampvar(x) 44.31072 44.90836 50.38668 62.14281 74.93704   100
##      var(x) 35.62815 36.60720 37.04430 37.88039 42.85260   100
```

With a median elapsed time of 50 milliseconds, our function takes only 36 percent more time than the optimized C version that has a median of 37 milliseconds.

The preceding exercise illustrates how code profiling can be used as part of a workflow to identify, prioritize, and fix performance issues in R programs. The rest of this book will cover techniques that we can use to solve specific performance problems.

Summary

In this chapter, we learned how to measure the execution time of R expressions using `system.time()`, `benchmark()` (from the `rbenchmark` package) and `microbenchmark()` (from the `microbenchmark` package). We examined how to profile the execution time and memory usage of different parts of an R program using `Rprof()` and `summaryRprof()` and to display the results in an intuitive visual form using the `proftools` package.

We also saw the role of OS-provided monitoring tools to understand the overall performance of R programs and how these system measures can provide clues about the performance bottlenecks that our R programs might be facing.

Finally, we learned how to apply the profiling techniques in a practical, iterative workflow to identify, prioritize and resolve performance related problems in an R code.

In the next chapter, we will learn some simple tweaks to improve R code so that it runs faster.

3
Simple Tweaks to Make R Run Faster

Improving the speed of an R code does not necessarily involve advanced optimization techniques like parallelizing the code or making it run in the database. Indeed, there are a number of simple tweaks that, while not always obvious, can make R run significantly faster. In this chapter, some of these tweaks are described. By no means do they capture all possible simple means to optimize the R code. However, they constitute some of the most fundamental, and hence often-encountered, opportunities to gain some speedups.

This chapter presents these tweaks in the order of decreasing generality — the more general ones are those found in almost all R codes, regardless of their application. Each tweak is accompanied by an example code that is intentionally kept simple so as not to obscure the explanation of the intended concept with unnecessary application-specific knowledge. In all these examples, artificial datasets are generated using random functions in R.

This chapter covers the following topics:

- Vectorization
- Use of built-in functions
- Preallocating memory
- Use of simpler data structures
- Use of hash tables for frequent lookups on large data
- Seeking fast alternative packages in CRAN

Vectorization

Most R users should have encountered this first tweak. In essence, vectorization allows R operators to take vectors as arguments for quick processing of multiple values. This is unlike some other programming languages such as C, C++, and Java, in which the processing of multiple values is usually done by iterating through and applying operators on each element of a vector (or array). R, being a flexible language, allows users to program using either iteration or vectorization. However, most of the time, iteration incurs significant and unnecessary computational cost because R is an interpreted, not compiled, language.

Take for example, the following simple code. Its goal is simply to calculate the square of every element in the random vector data. The first approach is to set up a for loop through every element of data and square it individually. Many would be tempted to take this approach because this is how it is done typically in other programming languages. Yet, a far more optimized approach in R is to apply the square operator on the data vector directly. This gives exactly the same output as the for loop, but much faster:

```
N <- 1E5
data <- sample(1:30, size=N, replace=T)
system.time({
  data_sq1 <- numeric(N)
  for(j in 1:N) {
    data_sq1[j] <- data[j]^2
  }
})
##   user   system elapsed
## 0.144    0.011   0.156
system.time(data_sq2 <- data^2)
##   user   system elapsed
##     0        0        0
```

The following table shows the performance gains as the vector size increases (in logarithmic scale) from 100,000 to 100,000,000. Notice that the compute time of the non-vectorized approach is about 200 times that of the vectorized approach, regardless of the vector size.

Vector size	100,000	1,000,000	10,000,000	100,000,000
Non-vectorized	120 ms	1.19 s	11.9 s	117 s
Vectorized	508 μs	5.67 ms	52.5 ms	583 ms

When R executes a code, it has to take many steps behind the scenes. One example is type checking. R objects such as vectors do not need to be strictly defined to be of a particular type, such as an integer or a character. One can append a character to an integer vector without triggering any error—R converts the vector into a character vector automatically. Every time an operator is applied on a vector, R needs to check the type of the vector only once, but with the use of the iteration approach, this type checking happens as many times as the number of iterations, which incurs some computational costs.

Use of built-in functions

As a programming language, R comes with low-level operators, such as basic arithmetic operators that can be used to construct more complex operators or functions. While R provides the flexibility to define functions, a performance comparison between an R function versus an equivalent function in a compiled language would almost always favor the latter. However, R and some CRAN packages provide a rich set of functions that are implemented in compiled languages such as C/C++. It is usually preferable to use these functions rather than to write custom R functions to perform the same task.

Consider a simple example of how to calculate the sums of the rows of the following random matrix `data`. A code to perform these functions can be constructed by calling the `apply()` function, and setting the margin to 1 (representing a row operation) and by setting the FUN (or function) argument to `sum`. Alternatively, R provides a built-in function for this purpose called `rowSums`. The computational time of the former approach, as measured by `system.time`, is 11 times longer than that of the latter approach, which is an optimized and precompiled C function:

```
data <- rnorm(1E4*1000)
dim(data) <- c(1E4,1000)
system.time(data_sum1 <- apply(data, 1, sum))
## user  system elapsed
## 0.241   0.053   0.294
system.time(data_sum2 <- rowSums(data))
## user  system elapsed
## 0.026   0.000   0.026
```

Speaking of optimized functions, our effort to improve the speed of an R code should not stop at precompiled functions that come with R. Over the years, the open source community has developed optimized libraries of specific functions that R can leverage. Take Basic Linear Algebra Subprograms (BLAS) for example (for more information refer to http://www.netlib.org/blas/). It was developed in the 1970s for Fortran and has since gained wider use by other languages (including R) because matrix operations make up the building blocks of many algorithms in various fields. There are now many implementations of BLAS, some of which include the capability to execute matrix operations in a multithreaded manner.

For example, the Mac OS X version of R comes enabled with BLAS. The implementation of BLAS that is used is the reference BLAS from R called libRblas.0.dylib. Mac OS X however comes with its own version of BLAS, libBLAS.dylib, which is optimized for its hardware. R can be configured to use the optimized BLAS by executing the following commands in Terminal:

```
$ cd /Library/Frameworks/R.framework/Resources/lib
$ ln -sf /System/Library/Frameworks/Accelerate.framework/Frameworks/
vecLib.framework/Versions/Current/libBLAS.dylib libRblas.dylib
```

To test the effect of using different BLAS libraries, the following R code performs a simple matrix multiplication on a large random matrix. Using R's default BLAS library, it took about 7 seconds for us to complete the task. After pointing R to the optimized BLAS, the same task was completed in about a tenth of the time:

```
data <- rnorm(1E7)
dim(data) <- c(1E4, 1E3)
system.time(data_mul <- t(data) %*% data)
##   user   system elapsed
## 7.123   0.015   7.136
system.time(data_mul <- t(data) %*% data) # with optimized BLAS
##   user   system elapsed
## 1.304   0.005   0.726
```

There are BLAS versions of Windows and Linux available for you to download. If R is compiled with an enabled BLAS, that is, by setting the configuration option to --enable-BLAS-shlib while compiling R from its source, swapping between BLAS versions is done in a similar manner as in Mac OS X: by replacing the default BLAS library file with the new one. In Windows, the default library is located in R_HOME\bin\x64\Rblas.dll; while in Linux, it is in R_HOME/lib/libRblas.so.

Preallocating memory

Most strongly typed programming languages like C, C++, and Java generally require a vector (or array) to be declared prior to any operation applied on it. This declaration in effect preallocates the memory space that the vector requires. There are special occasions where dynamic memory allocation is used, but this is seldom the first choice mainly because dynamic memory allocation slows down a program. Every time a vector is resized, the program needs to perform extra steps that include copying the vector to a larger or smaller memory block and deleting the old vector. These steps are not needed if the memory is preallocated.

When it comes to preallocating memory, R is no different from the other programming languages. However, being an interpreted language, it imposes less control, thus it is easy for users to overlook this—R will not throw any compilation error if a vector's memory is not preallocated. Nevertheless, not preallocating memory in R can result in significantly longer execution times, especially when the vector is large.

To demonstrate this, let's have a look at the following R code. It shows you two approaches to generate a series of random numbers, where each vector element is defined as the value of the previous element +/- a random integer between -5 to 5. The first approach (stores the results in data_series1) bypasses the preallocation of the vector's memory, that is, it starts with a vector of a single element and appends a new element at each iteration. The second approach (with results in data_series2) preallocates the memory by declaring a numeric vector of size N. The preallocated space, as represented by the vector's index, is filled in at every iteration. By preallocating the memory, the computation time on a vector of 10,000 elements is 10 times faster than the dynamic allocation. A benchmark exercise by varying the vector size, captured in the upcoming table, shows that while the computation time increases linearly when memory is preallocated, it increases super linearly when memory is dynamically allocated. It is critical for performance therefore to avoid unnecessary dynamic memory allocation in R:

```
N <- 1E4
data_series1 <- 1
system.time({
  for (j in 2:N) {
    data_series1 <- c(data_series1,
                      data_series1[j-1]+sample(-5:5, size=1))
  }
})
##   user  system elapsed
## 0.254   0.004   0.257
```

```
data_series2 <- numeric(N)
data_series2[1] <- 1
system.time({
  for (j in 2:N) {
    data_series2[j] <- data_series2[j-1]+sample(-5:5, size=1)
  }
})
##   user  system elapsed
## 0.066   0.003   0.068
```

Vector size	10	100	1000	10,000
Dynamic allocation	0	0.006	0.288	25.373
Preallocated	0.001	0.006	0.062	0.577

At this point, it is interesting to compare the `apply` family of functions versus loops in R. Most R users would be familiar with the `apply()` function and its variants, including `lapply()`, `sapply()`, and `tapply()`. They provide the means to perform the same operation repeatedly on individual elements of a collection (for example, `data.frame`, `list`, or `vector/matrix`). Effectively, the `apply` family serves as a possible substitute of looping in R, provided there are no dependencies between one iteration and another. Besides simplifying the expression (it is often possible to express a multiline `for` loop as a single line `apply()` call), the `apply` family offers the benefit of automatically taking care of the memory preallocation and other housekeeping activities like deleting loop indices.

But does `apply` offer performance advantages over looping? The following code offers an answer to this. Two different approaches are used to generate a list of normally distributed random vectors whose sizes are also randomly set to values between 1 and 30. The first approach uses a `for` loop while the second uses `lapply()`. Applying `system.time()` on both approaches shows that `lapply()` is significantly faster than the `for` loop:

```
N <- 1E5
data <- sample(1:30, size=N, replace=T)
data_rand1 <- list()
system.time(for(i in 1:N) data_rand1[[i]] <- rnorm(data[i]))
##   user  system elapsed
## 33.891   1.241   35.120
system.time(data_rand2 <- lapply(data, rnorm))
##   user  system elapsed
## 0.597   0.037   0.633
```

But note that the `for` loop is implemented naively without preallocating the memory. The following code modifies it now with the preallocated memory. Its computation time has significantly been reduced to be just a tenth of a second slower than `lapply()`:

```
data_rand3 <- vector("list", N)
system.time(for(i in 1:N) data_rand3[[i]] <- rnorm(data[i]))
##   user  system elapsed
## 0.737   0.036   0.773
```

To establish this more convincingly, the comparison was repeated using `microbenchmark()` to run each expression 100 times. The results indicate that `lapply()` offers a slight performance advantage over a `for` loop:

```
microbenchmark(data_rand2 <- lapply(data, rnorm),
               for(i in 1:N) data_rand3[[i]] <- rnorm(data[i]))
## Unit: milliseconds
##                                                  expr      min
##                data_rand2 <- lapply(data, rnorm) 441.1108
##   for (i in 1:N) data_rand3[[i]] <- rnorm(data[i]) 531.1212
##      lq     mean   median       uq      max neval
## 459.9666 498.1296 477.4583 517.4329 634.7849    100
## 555.8512 603.7997 581.5236 662.2536 745.4247    100
```

Based on this, the general view of replacing `for` loops with `apply` in R whenever possible is valid, but perhaps the performance gain would not be dramatic. In *Chapter 6, Simple Tweaks to Use Less RAM*, another benefit of `apply` will be discussed—that it reveals parts of R code that can be parallelized.

Use of simpler data structures

Many R users would agree that `data.frame` as a data structure is the workhorse of data analysis in R. It provides an intuitive way to represent a typical structured dataset with rows and columns representing observations and variables respectively. A `data.frame` object also allows more flexibility than a matrix by allowing variables of different types (such as character and numeric variables in a single `data.frame`). Furthermore, in cases where a `data.frame` stores only variables of the same type, basic matrix operations conveniently become applicable to it without any explicit coercing required. This convenience, however, can come with performance degradation.

Applying a matrix operation on a `data.frame` is slower than on a `matrix`. One of the reasons is that most matrix operations first coerce the `data.frame` into a `matrix` before performing the computation. For this reason, where possible, one should use a `matrix` in place of a `data.frame`. The next code demonstrates this point. The goal is simply to perform row summation on a matrix and its equivalent `data.frame` representation. Using a `matrix` representation results in about 3x speedup compared to using a `data.frame` representation:

```
data <- rnorm(1E4*1000)
dim(data) <- c(1E4,1000)
system.time(data_rs1 <- rowSums(data))
##   user   system elapsed
## 0.026    0.000   0.026
data_df <- data.frame(data)
system.time(data_rs2 <- rowSums(data_df))
##   user   system elapsed
## 0.060    0.015   0.076
```

In many cases of R however, the use of `data.frame` is unavoidable, for example, when a dataset has mixed variable types. In this case, there is also a simple tweak that can improve the speed of one of the most frequently used operations on a `data.frame`, subsetting. Subsetting a `data.frame` is commonly done by conditioning its rows (or columns) through a logical test as in the following code:

```
data <- rnorm(1E5*1000)
dim(data) <- c(1E5,1000)
data_df <- data.frame(data)
system.time(data_df[data_df$X100>0 & data_df$X200<0,])
##   user   system elapsed
## 2.436    0.221   2.656
```

An alternative to this is to wrap the condition by the `which` function. The speed is improved significantly as shown follows:

```
system.time(data_df[which(data_df$X100>0 & data_df$X200<0),])
##   user   system elapsed
## 0.245    0.086   0.331
```

Use of hash tables for frequent lookups on large data

One common task in data analysis is data lookup, which is often implemented via a list in R. For example, to look up customers' ages, we can define a list, say, cust_age, with values set to customer ages and names set to the corresponding customer names (or IDs), that is names(cust_age) <- cust_name. In this case, to look up John Doe's age, the following can be called: cust_age[["John_Doe"]]. However, the implementation of lists in R is not optimized for lookup; it incurs $O(N)$ time complexity to perform a lookup on a list of N elements. This means that the values indexed later in the list require more time to look up. As N grows, this effect gets stronger. When a program requires frequent lookups, the cumulative effect can be significant. An alternative to lists that offers a more optimized data lookup is a hash table. In R, this is available from the CRAN package *hash*. A hash table's lookup incurs $O(1)$ time complexity.

The next code demonstrates the benefit of lookups in hash tables over lists. It simulates 1,000 lookups from a random list and its equivalent hash table representation. The total computation time required for the list is 6.14 seconds, while for the hash table is 0.31 seconds. One trade-off is that it takes more time to generate a hash table than a list. But for a program that requires frequent lookups on large data, this overhead can be insignificant:

```
data <- rnorm(1E6)
data_ls <- as.list(data)
names(data_ls) <- paste("V", c(1:1E6), sep="")
index_rand <- sample(1:1E6, size=1000, replace=T)
index <- paste("V", index_rand, sep="")
list_comptime <- sapply(index, FUN=function(x){
  system.time(data_ls[[x]])[3]})
sum(list_comptime)
## [1] 6.144
library(hash)
data_h <- hash(names(data_ls), data)
hash_comptime <- sapply(index, FUN=function(x){
  system.time(data_h[[x]])[3]})
sum(hash_comptime)
## [1] 0.308
```

Seeking fast alternative packages in CRAN

One key advantage of R is its rich and active open source community, CRAN. As of the time of writing, there are over 6,000 R packages in CRAN. Given this, it is common that multiple packages offer the same functionalities. Some of these alternatives are designed specifically to improve the performance of a base or an existing CRAN package's performance. Others do not target performance improvement explicitly, but nevertheless achieve it as a by-product.

An example of an alternative fast package developed to achieve performance gains is the `fastcluster` package. It was developed to improve the speed of hierarchical clustering provided by the base package through the `hclust` function. Depending on how the distance matrix gets updated after every branch merging in the hierarchical clustering procedure, its time complexity can vary significantly. The `fastcluster` package is developed using an optimized C++ code that improves the speed significantly compared to the routines implemented in `hclust`. The following R code compares the performance of the two functions on a random matrix with 10,000 rows and 100 columns:

```
data <- rnorm(1E4*100)
dim(data) <- c(1E4,100)
dist_data <- dist(data)
system.time(hc_data <- hclust(dist_data))
##   user  system elapsed
## 3.488   0.200   4.081
library(fastcluster)
system.time(hc_data <- hclust(dist_data))
##   user  system elapsed
## 1.972   0.123   2.127
```

An example of a function that has more than one implementation, where one happens to be faster than the others as a by-product is **Principal Component Analysis (PCA)**. PCA is a dimensionality reduction technique that achieves its goal by projecting a dataset onto orthogonal axes (called principal components) that maximize the dataset's variance. The most common approach to PCA is via the Eigenvalue decomposition of the dataset's covariance matrix. But there are alternative methods. In R, two of these alternatives materialize in two PCA functions called `prcomp` and `princomp` (both are parts of the `stats` package). A quick comparison on a random matrix with 100,000 rows and 100 columns as in the following code demonstrates that `princomp` is close to 2x faster than `prcomp`:

```
data <- rnorm(1E5*100)
```

```
dim(data) <- c(1E5,100)
system.time(prcomp_data <- prcomp(data))
##   user   system elapsed
## 4.101    0.091   4.190
system.time(princomp_data <- princomp(data))
##   user   system elapsed
## 2.505    0.071   2.576
```

There are other examples of fast packages both explicitly and implicitly. They include:

- `fastmatch`: This provides a faster version of base R's `match` function
- `RcppEigen`: This includes a faster version of linear modeling `lm`
- `data.table`: This offers faster data manipulation operations compared to the standard `data.frame` operations
- `dplyr`: This offers a set of tools to manipulate data frame-like objects efficiently

Summary

This chapter described a few simple tweaks to improve the speed of an R code. Some of the tweaks are well known, but often overlooked in practice; others are less obvious. Regardless of their nature, and despite their simplicity, these low hanging fruits can offer significant performance gains and sometimes even more than the advanced optimization discussed in subsequent chapters. As such, these tweaks should be taken as the first steps in order to optimize an R code.

In the next chapter, we will see how to take R's performance even further by using compiled code.

4
Using Compiled Code for Greater Speed

So far, we have looked at how to optimize the computational performance of an R code. What if, after optimizing the code, it still runs too slowly? In this chapter, we will look at how to overcome the performance limitations caused by on-the-fly interpretation of an R code using a compiled code. Many CRAN packages use compiled code to offer optimum performance, so a simple way to take advantage of a compiled code is to use these packages. Sometimes, however, a specific task needs to be performed for which no package exists. It is useful to know how to write a compiled code for R in order to make R programs run faster.

We will first see how to compile R code before its execution, then we will explore how to integrate compiled languages like C/C++ into R so that we can run R programs at native CPU speed.

This chapter covers the following topics:

- Compiling an R code before execution
- Using compiled languages in R

Compiling R code before execution

In *Chapter 1, Understanding R's Performance – Why Are R Programs Sometimes Slow?* we saw how R, being an interpreted language, has to parse and evaluate code every time an R program is run. This takes a lot of CPU time and slows down the execution of R programs. R provides the `compiler` package to somewhat reduce this issue. The functions in this package allow us to compile R code beforehand and save R a step or two when we execute the code. Let's see how this works.

Compiling functions

Let's define a `mov.avg()` function that calculates the moving average of a numeric series:

```
# Compute the n-period moving average of x
mov.avg <- function(x, n=20) {
    total <- numeric(length(x) - n + 1)
    for (i in 1:n) {
        total <- total + x[i:(length(x) - n + i)]
    }
    total / n
}
```

Given a numeric vector x and period n, we first calculate the n element's window sum of the elements of x. For example, if x is [1, 2, 1, 3, 5] and n is 2, then we calculate `total` as [1+2, 2+1, 1+3, 3+5] = [3, 3, 4, 8]. We do this by looping n times over x, selecting a moving window of the elements of x, and adding those elements to `total`. Finally, we compute the moving average by dividing `total` by n.

To compile the function, we will use the `cmpfun()` function in the `compiler` package. The compilation functions provided by the `compiler` package operate on four different levels of optimization, numbered 0 to 3; the higher the number, the more the compiled code is optimized for performance.

Let's compile `mov.avg()` at different levels to see the differences in execution time. Here, we create four copies of the `mov.avg()` function compiled at different levels of optimization by passing the `optimize` argument to `cmpfun()`:

```
library(compiler)
mov.avg.compiled0 <- cmpfun(mov.avg, options=list(optimize=0))
mov.avg.compiled1 <- cmpfun(mov.avg, options=list(optimize=1))
mov.avg.compiled2 <- cmpfun(mov.avg, options=list(optimize=2))
mov.avg.compiled3 <- cmpfun(mov.avg, options=list(optimize=3))
```

Next, we benchmark the performance of the original `mov.avg()` function and the four compiled versions by computing the 20-period moving average of a numeric vector with 100 elements:

```
library(microbenchmark)
x <- runif(100)
bench <- microbenchmark(mov.avg(x),
```

```
                    mov.avg.compiled0(x),
                    mov.avg.compiled1(x),
                    mov.avg.compiled2(x),
                    mov.avg.compiled3(x))
bench
## Unit: microseconds
##                      expr    min      lq  median      uq      max
##                mov.avg(x) 34.257 37.6865 41.3630 72.3015  131.101
##  mov.avg.compiled0(x) 33.500 36.9065 41.9995 72.8770 2605.917
##  mov.avg.compiled1(x) 34.643 36.8615 41.0650 71.8480  117.632
##  mov.avg.compiled2(x) 24.050 25.9040 28.3060 51.8685 3693.741
##  mov.avg.compiled3(x) 23.399 24.6540 27.7670 49.6385   89.595
##  neval
##    100
##    100
##    100
##    100
##    100
```

Looking at the median execution times, the original function took 41.4 µs. The compiled functions at optimization levels 0 and 1 took about the same time, coming in at 42.0 µs and 41.1 µs respectively. However those at optimization levels 2 and 3 performed well, at 28.3 µs and 27.8 µs. They reduced the execution time by 32 percent and 33 percent respectively.

The minimum lower quartile and upper quartile statistics shows a similar pattern with mov.avg.compiled2() and mov.avg.compiled3() executing in less time than mov.avg(), mov.avg.compiled0(), and mov.avg.compiled1().

We should not rely on the maximum statistics because it can be unstable, producing a wide range of values every time we run microbenchmark(). This is due to the outliers when R's garbage collection takes place, or when the execution of the functions are slowed down by other processes competing for CPU time.

The following chart shows the distributions of the benchmarking results in an intuitive visual form.

Generate an intuitive visualization of the benchmarking results by using the `autoplot()` function. The `ggplot2` package is needed for this:

```
library(ggplot2)
autoplot(bench)
```

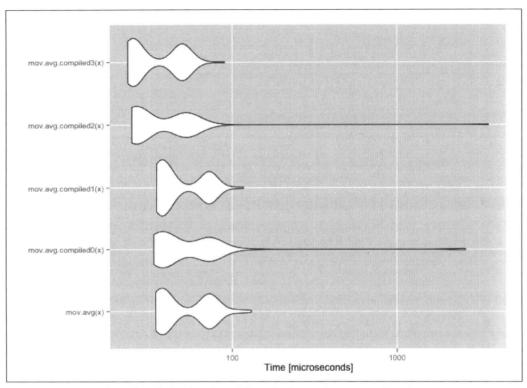

Autoplot of microbenchmark() results for moving average functions

The performance gain when R code is compiled depends on what kinds of R expressions are contained in the code. In our example, we achieved modest performance gains because the `for` loop and the arithmetic operations in the `mov.avg()` function could be optimized. However, compiling code that mostly calls other functions that have already been optimized for performance (such as `sum()`) would not result in significant performance gains.

The `compiler` package provides different functions to compile different types of R code:

- `cmpfun()` compiles an R function.
- `compile()` compiles an R expression.
- `cmpfile()` compiles an R expression stored in a file.

Just-in-time (JIT) compilation of R code

R also supports **just-in-time (JIT) compilation**. When JIT compilation is enabled, R will automatically compile any code that is executed without explicitly having called one of the `compile` functions. This is convenient, as any existing R code can enjoy the performance gains of code compilation without any modification.

To activate JIT compilation, use the `enableJIT()` function in the `compiler` package:

```
library(compiler)
enableJIT(level=3)
```

The `level` argument tells R how much code to compile before execution. Valid values for `level` are:

- `0`: It disables JIT.
- `1`: It compiles functions before their first use.
- `2`: In addition, it compiles functions before they are duplicated. This is useful for some packages like lattice that store functions in lists.
- `3`: It compiles loops before they are executed.

Let's benchmark the (uncompiled) `mov.avg()` function with the JIT compilation:

```
microbenchmark(mov.avg(x))
## Unit: microseconds
##         expr    min     lq median     uq      max neval
##   mov.avg(x) 23.164 24.009 24.519 25.128 6097.067   100
```

The JIT compilation reduced the median execution time of `mov.avg()` from 41.4 µs to 24.5 µs — a 41 percent improvement!

JIT compilation can also be enabled by setting the `R_ENABLE_JIT` environment in the operating system before starting R. The value of `R_ENABLE_JIT` should be set to the value of the `level` argument.

Using compiled languages in R

Code compilation can provide modest gains in computational performance, but there are limits to these gains because the compiled code still needs to be evaluated by R in a dynamic fashion. For example, we explained in *Chapter 3, Simple Tweaks to Make R Run Faster*, how R, being a **dynamically typed** language, needs to check the type of an object before applying any operations. In the case of `mov.avg()`, every time R encounters the + operator, it needs to check that x is a numeric vector, as it could have been modified between each iteration of the `for` loop. In contrast, a **statically typed** language performs these checks at compile time, resulting in much faster run time performance.

For this and many other reasons, R's dynamic nature poses barriers to computational performance. The only way to break through these barriers is to turn to compiled languages such as C and use them from within R. This section assumes that you have some basic knowledge of compiled languages such as C/C++, including pointers and arrays.

Prerequisites

In order to compile the examples in this chapter, a set of development tools, including a C/C++ compiler are needed.

Windows users should download and install `Rtools` from `http://cran.r-project.org/bin/windows/Rtools/`. Pick the version of `Rtools` that corresponds to your version of R. Be sure to select the **Package authoring installation** and **Edit the system PATH** options in the installation wizard.

On Mac OS X, download and install the *Xcode Command Line Tools*. If you are using Mac OS X 10.9 Mavericks or a later version, simply run `xcode-select –install` in terminal. For earlier versions of Mac OS X, create a developer account at `http://developer.apple.com/`. Then sign in, go to `https://developer.apple.com/downloads/index.action` and search for command-line tools for Xcode for your OS version.

Most Linux distributions offer an easy way to install the standard development tools; consult the documentation of your distribution for instructions. If you are using Debian or Ubuntu, you can just install `r-base-dev` to get all the tools you need.

Including compiled code inline

The `inline` CRAN package allows us to embed C, C++, Objective-C, Objective-C++, and Fortran code within R. This is handy for speeding up small R functions with a bit of compiled code.

Here is an example of how to implement `mov.avg()` in C using the `inline` package:

```
library(inline)
mov.avg.inline <- cfunction(
    sig=signature(x="numeric", n="integer"),
    body="
        /* Coerce arguments to the correct types needed.
            x needs to be a numeric vector (type REALSXP), and n
            needs to be an integer vector (type INTSXP). */
        SEXP x2 = PROTECT(coerceVector(x, REALSXP));
        SEXP n2 = PROTECT(coerceVector(n, INTSXP));

        /* Create accessors to the actual data being pointed to by
            the two SEXP's. */
        double *x_p = REAL(x2);
        int n_val = asInteger(n2);

        // Vector lengths
        int x_len = length(x2);
        int res_len = x_len - n_val + 1;

        /* Create and initialize a numeric vector (type REALSXP)
            of length res_len, using allocVector().
            Since memory is allocated, use PROTECT to protect the
            object from R's garbage collection. */
        SEXP res = PROTECT(allocVector(REALSXP, res_len));
        double *res_p = REAL(res);
        for (int i = 0; i < res_len; i++) {
            res_p[i] = 0;
        }

        // Compute window sum
        for (int j = 0; j < n_val; j++) {
            for (int k = 0; k < res_len; k++) {
                res_p[k] += x_p[j + k];
            }
        }

        // Compute moving average
        for (int l = 0; l < res_len; l++) {
            res_p[l] /= n_val;
        }

        // Unprotect allocated memory and return results
```

```
            UNPROTECT(3);
            return res;
    ',
    language="C"
    )
```

We load the `inline` package and define `mov.avg.inline()` using `cfunction()`. A number of arguments are taken by `cfunction()` (look up the documentation for more details), but we need only three here:

- `sig=signature(x="numeric", n="integer")`: This defines the signature of the function. In this case, it will look like `mov.avg.inline(x, n)`, where x has the numeric class and the n has integer class.

- `body`: The `body` argument contains the code for the function's body in the programming language of your choice.

- `language="C"`: This specifies the programming language of the code in body. Valid values are `C`, `C++`, `Fortran`, `F95`, `ObjectiveC`, and `ObjectiveC++`.

The first step of the function is to make sure that the arguments supplied to the function are of the correct type by calling `coerceVector()`. This function returns an SEXP (s-expression) pointer, which is how all R objects are represented in C and C++. These pointers point to SEXPREC (s-expression) record structures that store the data along with some header information. The first two lines of code define two new SEXP variables, x2 and n2, that store pointers to new R objects created by coercing the function arguments.

Because `coerceVector()` creates new data structures in memory to store the data in the specified types, we wrap the calls to `coerceVector()` in the macro function `PROTECT()`, which protects the newly created data structures from R's garbage collection mechanisms. This is necessary because R does not know when variables are no longer needed in C, and might be overzealous in freeing memory for objects that are still needed. `PROTECT()` needs to be called every time memory is allocated for a new R object.

Now x2 and n2 contain SEXP pointers of R objects that represent the coerced arguments. Because x2 and n2 point to SEXPREC structures, we still do not have direct access to the C arrays that store the data. There are a couple of ways to get access to the data. In `double *x_p = REAL(x2);`, the `REAL()` macro returns a `double*` pointing to the first element of the double array. The `int n_val = asInteger(n2);` declaration takes a different approach by calling the `asInteger()` convenience function to return the first integer value in the array pointed to by n2. Notice the difference here; x_p is a pointer to a double array while n_val is an integer containing the actual value of the argument. Both styles of access to the R data can be used depending on which is more convenient.

Next, we compute the length `res_len` of the numeric vector in which we will store the results, and create the vector using `allocVector()`. Again, this is wrapped in `PROTECT()` because memory is being allocated for a new object. The result of this expression is a SEXP pointing to the new R numeric vector. `REAL(res)` provides access to the underlying C double array, as before.

The next pair of nested `for` loops computes the window sum with the `n_val` period. Then, the moving average is computed by dividing each element of the results array by `n_val`.

Before returning the results, there is some housekeeping that is required. `UNPROTECT(3)` tells R that the three objects for which memory was allocated in C, do not need protection from garbage collection anymore. The argument to `UNPROTECT()` must match the number of calls to `PROTECT()` in the function. In this case, it is likely that the the garbage collector will free the memory for `x2` and `n2`. The `res` object, however, is passed back to R, where the normal garbage collection mechanisms apply.

Let's do a simple test to ensure that our code works correctly by calling the original `mov.avg()` function alongside `mov.avg.inline()` and ensuring that the values match:

```
x <- runif(100)
all(mov.avg(x, 20) == mov.avg.inline(x, 20))
## [1] TRUE
```

How much quicker will the C code run than the original uncompiled R function? This is shown, as follows:

```
microbenchmark(mov.avg(x, 20), mov.avg.inline(x, 20))
## Unit: microseconds
##                    expr    min     lq  median      uq      max
##          mov.avg(x, 20) 32.909 34.113 34.8240 35.6975 130.155
## mov.avg.inline(x, 20)  1.347  1.423  1.5535  1.7015  14.169
## neval
##    100
##    100
```

The C code took an average of just 1.55 µs compared with 34.8 µs for the R code—a 96 percent reduction in execution time! Even the maximum execution time in C (14.2 µs) is less than half of the minimum execution time in R (32.9 µs). These savings of a few microseconds might not seem like much, but the difference becomes significant when we have to process larger datasets or compute moving averages with larger periods:

```
y <- runif(1e7)
microbenchmark(mov.avg(y, 20), mov.avg.inline(y, 20))
## Unit: milliseconds
```

```
##                       expr       min        lq    median        uq
##        mov.avg(y, 20) 2046.4608 2198.6103 2252.7003 2318.721
## mov.avg.inline(y, 20)  272.8686  280.2837  283.3647  292.587
##        max neval
## 3606.3911    100
##  374.0193    100
```

When the data contains 10 million numbers, the difference is more pronounced; over 2 seconds in R and only 0.28 seconds in C. In some business contexts, every millisecond counts, and a latency of 2 seconds is not acceptable. In such situations, writing key pieces of data processing code in a compiled language like C or Fortran and embedding them into R using `inline` will give a huge boost to computational performance.

Calling external compiled code

We have seen how to use a compiled language to define functions in R. When we want to implement more complex functionality using compiled code, such as creating entire R packages or linking to external libraries, it might be easier to develop the code externally and to call it from R.

R provides a few interfaces to call the external compiled code:

- `.C()`: This calls C or C++ code with a maximum of 65 arguments. Type checking and coercion must be done in R before calling the C function. Functions called by `.C()` should not return any values; instead, when the function is called, the results stored by data structures should be supplied to the function. For example, if we were to implement `mov.avg()` using the `.C()` interface, the function call might look like `.C("mov_avg_C", as.numeric(x), as.integer(n), numeric(length(x) - n + 1))`.

- `.Fortran()`: This is similar to `.C()` except it calls `Fortran` code.

- `.Call()`: This also calls C or C++ code with a maximum of 65 arguments. Type checking and coercion can be done in R or in C/C++ (as in the `mov.avg.inline()` example). Functions called by `.Call()` can return an R object. If multiple return values are needed, an R list can be returned. For example, `ma <- .Call("mov_avg_C", x, n)`.

- `.External()`: This is similar to `.Call()` except all arguments are passed in a single SEXP. As a result, functions called with `.External()` can accept a variable number of arguments and a practically unlimited number of arguments.

The functions provided by the `inline` package are actually wrappers for some of the lower-level interfaces that make it easier for developers to embed a compiled code in R.

It is beyond the scope of this book to explain in detail how to use these interfaces. To learn more, read the *System and foreign language interfaces* and *The R API* sections of the *Writing R Extensions* manual (for more information visit `http://cran.r-project.org/doc/manuals/r-release/R-exts.html`).

 For Java programmers, the `rJava` package on CRAN provides an interface to Java code.

Instead, we would like to introduce the `Rcpp` package that provides a convenient, higher-level API to the `.Call()` interface for C++ code. Here is the moving average function implemented using `Rcpp`. Save this code in the `mov_avg_Rcpp.cpp` file:

```cpp
#include <Rcpp.h>

// [[Rcpp::export]]
Rcpp::NumericVector mov_avg_Rcpp(Rcpp::NumericVector x,
                                 int n=20) {
    // Vector lengths
    int x_len = x.size();
    int res_len = x_len - n + 1;

    // Create and initialize vector for results
    Rcpp::NumericVector res(res_len);

    // Compute window sum
    for (int j = 0; j < n; j++) {
        for (int k = 0; k < res_len; k++) {
            res[k] += x[j + k];
        }
    }

    // Compute moving average
    for (int l = 0; l < res_len; l++) {
        res[l] /= n;
    }

    // Return results
    return res;
}
```

The first line `#include <Rcpp.h>` imports the headers required to use `Rcpp` classes and functions. The comment `// [[Rcpp::export]]` is an `Rcpp` attribute. It tells `Rcpp` that the following function should be exported to R.

`SEXP` pointers are not used in `mov_avg_Rcpp()`. Instead, `Rcpp` provides classes that represent the standard R classes. We can even specify that `n` is a single integer and not an integer vector. Whenever `mov_avg_Rcpp()` is called from R, `Rcpp` will automatically check that the supplied arguments are of the correct type.

Notice that there are no calls to `PROTECT()` or `UNPROTECT()` here. When `Rcpp::NumericVector res(res_len);` creates a new numeric vector for the results, `Rcpp` takes care of the memory allocation and protection from garbage collection. It even initializes the values of the new vector to zeroes.

`Rcpp` also provides direct access to the data in the `x` argument and the results vector `res` without having to ask for pointers to the data.

Using `Rcpp`, we can write more succinct and readable code than possible using the native `.C()` or `.Call()` interfaces.

Let's now see how to call this function from within R. Besides loading the `Rcpp` library, the only other thing to do is to call `sourceCpp()`, which will compile the C++ code and export the function to R:

```
library(Rcpp)
sourceCpp('mov_avg_Rcpp.cpp")
```

Now, we can call `mov_avg_Rcpp()` and benchmark it against our previous versions:

```
x <- runif(100)
microbenchmark(mov.avg(x, 20),
               mov.avg.inline(x, 20),
               mov_avg_Rcpp(x, 20))
## Unit: microseconds
##                   expr    min     lq median      uq     max
##         mov.avg(x, 20) 33.902 35.779 37.472 49.7340 101.325
## mov.avg.inline(x, 20)  1.327  1.513  1.718  1.9655  14.129
##   mov_avg_Rcpp(x, 20)  2.382  2.727  2.874  3.9705  11.424
## neval
##   100
##   100
##   100
```

The Rcpp version runs a little slower than the inline version, but it is still much faster than our pure R code. It provides a good level of performance with a much simpler API than the other interfaces provided by R.

Rcpp provides many more features than we can cover in this book such as package authoring tools, the sugar functions for common operations such as vector operations, and more. For more details, code examples, and resources, look up the Rcpp website at http://www.rcpp.org/. One of the creators of Rcpp, Dirk Eddelbuettel, has also written the *Seamless R and C++ Integration with Rcpp (use R!)* book that provides a comprehensive guide.

Considerations for using compiled code

There are a few things to bear in mind while using compiled code in R. We will explain the common ones here; the *Writing R Extensions* manual provides a comprehensive treatment of these topics.

R APIs

The C functions and macros used so far are from the header file Rinternals.h, found in R_INCLUDE_DIR which defaults to R_HOME/include in any standard R installation. This file, together with R.h and other header files in R_INCLUDE_DIR, provides various APIs for C/C++ code to interface with R. Together they provide a rich set of functions for:

- Manipulating R objects (for example, sorting vectors)
- Managing memory allocation and deallocation
- Math (for example, trigonometric functions)
- Mathematical constants
- Random number generation
- Statistical distributions (for example, rnorm and punif)
- BLAS, LAPACK, and LINPACK linear algebra routines
- And much more

It is worthwhile to explore these files in order to see which functionality is available for C/C++ code. Some of these can be called from Fortran as well. The *Organization of header files* section of *Writing R Extensions* describes each header file.

R data types versus native data types

While working in compiled languages, it is useful to know how R types map to different native data types, as shown in the following table:

R storage mode	C type	Fortran type
logical	int *	INTEGER
integer	int *	INTEGER
double	double *	DOUBLE PRECISION
complex	Rcomplex *	DOUBLE COMPLEX
character	char **	CHARACTER*255
raw	unsigned char *	none

When dealing with SEXP pointers in C/C++ or type classes in Rcpp, here are the most commonly used types (look up the documentation for R or Rcpp for a complete list):

R type	SEXP Type	Rcpp type
numeric	REALSXP	NumericVector / NumericMatrix
integer	INTSXP	IntegerVector / IntegerMatrix
complex	CPLXSXP	ComplexVector / ComplexMatrix
logical	LGLSXP	LogicalVector / LogicalMatrix
character	STRSXP	CharacterVector / CharacterMatrix
list	VECSXP	List
data.frame	none	DataFrame

Creating R objects and garbage collection

We have seen how R objects can be created and memory can be allocated for them by calling allocVector() and coerceVector(). Rinternals.h defines other memory allocation functions as well, such as allocList() and allocArray(). Any call to the alloc*() functions or coerceVector() needs to be wrapped in PROTECT().

In the mov.avg.inline() example, UNPROTECT() is used to remove garbage collection protection right before returning the results. UNPROTECT() can also be called at any point in a function to allow the garbage collector to release R objects that are no longer needed. The protection mechanism is stack-based, so UNPROTECT(n) removes the protection from the last n objects that were protected. Alternatively, UNPROTECT_PTR(p) can be used to unprotect the specific object that SEXP p points to, even if it is not at the top of the stack.

In complex C/C++ code that creates many R objects, it is good practice to unprotect them once they are not needed, so that the garbage collector can do its job efficiently. However, it is the programmer's responsibility to make sure that those unprotected objects are never used again in the code, to prevent any memory errors.

Finally, always remember to match the number of the PROTECT() calls with the total number of objects unprotected by UNPROTECT() or UNPROTECT_PTR().

Allocating memory for non-R objects

Sometimes, memory is needed to store the results of intermediate computations that do not need to be accessed from R. R provides two ways of allocating memory like this in C/C++.

The first method, **transient storage allocation**, allows you to allocate memory that is automatically reclaimed by R at the end of the call to .C(), .Call() or .External(). To do this, use the char *R_alloc(size_t n, int size) function, which allocates n units of size bytes each and returns a pointer to the allocated memory. A typical usage might look like:

```
int *x = (int *) R_alloc(100, sizeof(int));
```

There is no need to free the allocated memory within the C/C++ function, as R will take care of that when the function execution ends.

The **user-controlled memory** mechanism provides more control over the allocation and freeing of memory. This allows memory to be freed between different parts of C/C++ code. For example, in an iterative algorithm where each stage of computation produces large amounts of intermediate data, memory from previous iterations can be freed to ensure that there is sufficient free memory to complete future iterations. There are three functions in this interface:

- type* Calloc(size_t n, type): This allocates memory of the specified size and type

- type* Realloc(any *p, size_t n, type): This changes the size of the memory allocated at *p to the specified size and type

- void Free(any *p): This frees the memory at *p

These functions are analogous to the C functions calloc(), realloc(), and free(), with additional error handling by R. If they return, then the memory has been successfully allocated or freed.

Summary

In this chapter, we covered a variety of techniques to leverage code in compiled languages for a near-native CPU performance. While the examples focused on C and C++, similar approaches can be used with Fortran or Java.

We first saw how compiling an R code before its execution by using the `compile` package can provide modest performance gains, especially for code with many loops and basic operations. JIT compilation does the same automatically for executing any R code. There is a limit, however, to how much an R code can be optimized because R is a dynamic language at its core.

Looking beyond R, we used C and C++ to achieve dramatic performance improvements. We learned how to define a C function from within R, using the `inline` package, and how to use Rcpp to call an external C++ function from R.

In the process, we learned about how R represents different types of data in C/C++ using SEXP pointers and SEXPREC record structures, and how to manipulate R objects using these constructs. We also learned about the intricacies of allocating memory, freeing memory, and garbage collection while working in C/C++.

Finally, we took a quick tour of the R APIs that provide rich R functionality from within C, C++, or Fortran.

This chapter covered advanced techniques to achieve optimized computational performance in R, using compiled languages. These techniques allow R programmers to tap into the power and speed of compiled languages while enjoying the simplicity and flexibility of R as a data processing environment. The huge performance gains from using compiled languages come with an equally huge responsibility to understand in detail how these techniques work, so that they can be used safely and effectively. Whole books could be written on this topic; we encourage you to look up other resources including the *Writing R Extensions* manual for a deeper and more comprehensive treatment.

In the next chapter, we will look at how to leverage the computing power of **Graphics Processing Units (GPUs)** for certain types of computations.

5

Using GPUs to Run R Even Faster

In this chapter, we will look at another means to speed up the execution of an R code using a technology that is often untapped, although it is part of most computers—the **Graphics Processing Unit (GPU)**, otherwise known as a graphics card. When we think of a GPU, we often think of the amazing graphics it can produce. In fact, GPUs are powered by technologies with highly parallel processing capabilities that are like the top supercomputers in the world. In the past, programming with GPUs was very difficult. However, in the last few years, this barrier has been removed with GPU programming platforms like CUDA and OpenCL that make programming with GPUs accessible for many programmers. Better still, the R community has developed a few packages for R users to leverage the computing power of GPUs.

To run the examples in this chapter, you will need an NVIDIA GPU with CUDA capabilities.

This chapter covers:

- General purpose computing on GPUs
- R and GPUs
- Fast statistical modeling in R with `gputools`

General purpose computing on GPUs

Historically, GPUs were designed and used to render high-resolution graphics such as for video games. To be able to render millions of pixels every second, GPUs utilize a highly parallel architecture that specializes in the types of computations required to render graphics. At a high level, the architecture of a GPU is similar to that of a CPU—it has its own multi-core processor and memory. However, because GPUs are not designed for general computation, individual cores are much simpler with slower clock speeds and limited support for complex instructions, compared to CPUs. In addition, they typically have less RAM than CPUs. To achieve real-time rendering, most GPU computations are done in a highly parallel manner, with many more cores than CPUs—a modern GPU might have more than 2,000 cores. Given that one core can run multiple threads, it is possible to run tens of thousands of parallel threads on a GPU.

In 1990s, programmers began to realize that certain computations outside of graphics rendering can benefit from the highly parallel architecture of GPUs. Remember the embarrassingly parallel nature of vectorized operations in R from *Chapter 3*, *Simple Tweaks to Make R Run Faster*; imagine the potential speedup if they were done simultaneously by thousands of GPU cores. This awareness gave rise to general purpose computing on GPUs (GPGPU).

But it was challenging to program GPUs. Using low-level interfaces provided by standards like DirectX and OpenGL, programmers had to trick the GPUs to compute on numbers as if they were rendering graphics. Realizing this challenge, efforts sprung up to develop proper programming languages and the supporting architectures for GPGPU. The chief outcomes from these efforts are two technologies called CUDA, developed by NVIDIA, and OpenCL, developed by Apple and now maintained by Khronos. While CUDA is proprietary and works only on NVIDIA GPUs, OpenCL is brand agnostic and is even able to support other accelerators like **Field Programmable Gate Arrays (FPGAs)**.

R and GPUs

The R community has developed a few packages for R programmers to leverage GPUs. The vectorized nature of R makes the use of GPUs a natural fit. The packages vary in the level of encapsulation and hence the required familiarity with the native CUDA or OpenCL languages. A selection of R packages for GPU programming are listed here:

- gputools: This provides R functions that wrap around GPU-based algorithms for common operations, such as linear models and matrix algebra. It requires CUDA, and hence an NVIDIA GPU.

- gmatrix: This provides the gmatrix and gvector classes to represent matrices and vectors respectively in NVIDIA GPUs. It also provides functions for common matrix operations such as matrix algebra, and random number generation and sorting.

- RCUDA: This provides a low-level interface to load and call a CUDA kernel from an R session. Using RCUDA requires a good understanding of the CUDA language, but allows more flexibility and code optimization. More information about t can be found at http://www.omegahat.org/RCUDA/.

- OpenCL: This is similar to RCUDA, but interfaces with OpenCL. It caters to users that have non-NVIDIA GPUs like ATI, Intel, or AMD GPUs.

Other CRAN packages are available for more specialized functions on GPUs, such as linear regression. For a list of these packages, see the GPUs section of *CRAN Task View: High-Performance and Parallel Computing with R*, maintained by Dirk Eddelbuettel on the CRAN website at http://cran.r-project.org/web/views/HighPerformanceComputing.html.

In this chapter, we will focus only on gputools and use a few examples from this package to illustrate how GPUs can speed up computations in R.

Installing gputools

These are the steps to install gputools:

1. Make sure that your computer has a CUDA-enabled GPU card. For the list of CUDA-enabled GPUs, refer to https://developer.nvidia.com/cuda-gpus.

2. Download and install CUDA toolkit from https://developer.nvidia.com/cuda-downloads.

3. Set a few environment variables as specified in the gputools installation note http://cran.r-project.org/web/packages/gputools/INSTALL.

4. Open an R session and run install.packages("gputools").

If you do not have an NVIDIA GPU with CUDA capabilities, **Amazon Web Services (AWS)** offers GPU instances, called g2.2xlarge instances, that come with (at the time of writing) NVIDIA GRID K520 GPUs with 1,536 CUDA cores and 4 GB of video memory. You can use these instances together with **Amazon Machine Images (AMIs)** provided by NVIDIA that are preloaded with the CUDA toolkit and drivers. Both Windows and Linux AMIs are available at https://aws.amazon.com/marketplace/seller-profile/ref=sp_mpg_product_vendor?ie=UTF8&id=c568fe05-e33b-411c-b0ab-047218431da9. For this chapter, we used the Linux AMI version 2014.03.2.

Fast statistical modeling in R with gputools

gputools provides a convenient way to execute statistical functions on a GPU, without CUDA programming. All the heavy lifting, including copying data from RAM to GPU memory and setting the number of cores to use have been encapsulated within the functions (in fact, gputools relies on the well-encapsulated CUBLAS library, which provides linear algebra functions for GPUs). For example, to perform linear modeling on the mtcars dataset on a CPU, we use the lm(): lm(mpg~cyl+disp+hp, data=mtcars) function. To run it on a GPU, we call the gpuLm() function from gputools: gpuLm(mpg~cyl+disp+hp, data=mtcars). The output of gpuLm() follows the same format as lm().

To demonstrate the speedup that we can expect from a GPU, we will calculate Kendall correlations on random datasets having 100 variables. We will use a varying number of observations from 100, 200, … to 500 records in order to observe the speedup in comparison to the CPU version. The code is as follows:

```
library(gputools)
A <- lapply(c(1:5), function(x) {
    matrix(rnorm((x*1e2) * 1e2), 1e2, (x*1e2))})
cpu_k_time <- sapply(A, function(x) {
    system.time(cor(x=x, method="kendall"))[[3]]})
gpu_k_time <- sapply(A, function(x) {
    system.time(gpuCor(x=x, method="kendall"))[[3]]})
K <- data.frame(cpu=cpu_k_time, gpu=gpu_k_time)
```

We tested this code on an NVIDIA GRID K520 GPU from AWS; the performance you get depends on your GPU. The computational times are plotted on the following figure. We see that the CPU version of the cor() correlation function scales super linearly with the number of records. On the other hand, the GPU version shows a very small increase in computation time as the number of records increases, as evident from the almost flat red line.

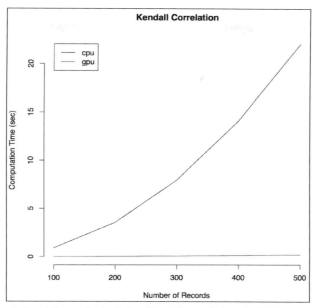

Computational times of calculating Kendall correlations in GPU versus CPU

Next, we will run timing comparisons for a few other functions available in
gputools: linear model (gpuLm()), generalized linear model (gpuGlm()), distance
matrix calculation (gpuDist()), and matrix multiplication (gpuMatMult()). The
datasets used for these tests have 1,000 observations and 1,000 variables, except for
gpuLm, where a dataset with 10,000 observations and 1,000 variables is used. The
microbenchmark() function is used to compare the execution times of the CPU
and GPU versions of these algorithms:

```
library(microbenchmark)
A <- matrix(rnorm(1e7), 1e4, 1e3)
A_df <- data.frame(A)
A_df$label <- rnorm(1e4)
microbenchmark(lm(label~., data=A_df),
               gpuLm(label~., data=A_df),
               times=30L)
## Unit: seconds
##              expr       min        lq     median        uq
##    lm(formu,...) 18.153458 18.228136 18.264231 18.274046
## gpuLm(formu,...)  9.310136  9.424152  9.467559  9.507548
##       max
## 18.32938
## 10.25019

A <- matrix(rnorm(1e6), 1e3, 1e3)
```

```
A_df <- data.frame(A)
A_df$label <- rbinom(1e3, size=1, prob=0.5)
microbenchmark(glm(label~., data=A_df, family=binomial),
               gpuGlm(label~., data=A_df, family=binomial),
               times=30L)
## Unit: seconds
##              expr       min       lq    median        uq       max
##    glm(formu,...) 23.64777 23.68571 23.73135 23.82055 24.07102
## gpuGlm(formu,...) 15.14166 15.30302 15.42091 15.50876 15.71143


microbenchmark(dist(A), gpuDist(A), times=30L)
## Unit: milliseconds
##       expr        min         lq     median         uq        max
##    dist(A) 11113.4842 11141.2138 11167.81 11194.852 11287.2603
## gpuDist(A)   191.1447   203.6862   222.79   229.408   239.9834


B <- matrix(rnorm(1E6), 1E3, 1E3)
microbenchmark(A%*%B, gpuMatMult(A, B), times=30L)
## Unit: milliseconds
##              expr       min        lq    median        uq
##             A%*%B 921.68863 934.64234 945.74926 955.33485
## gpuMatMult(A,B)  33.28274  33.59875  33.70138  37.35431
##               max
## 1029.75887
##   38.29123
```

The test results show the power of using GPU computations in R. However, just like any other parallel program, not all functions will enjoy faster performance when executed in a GPU. For example, running the correlation comparison for Pearson's correlations (by changing the `method` argument from `kendall` to `pearson`), the GPU performs slower than the CPU as shown in the upcoming figure. Due to the extra sorting operations required by the Kendall correlation, it is known to be much more computationally intensive than the Pearson correlation (our benchmark here shows that computing the Kendall correlation is hundreds of times slower than computing the Pearson correlation). However, it seems that this implementation of the Kendall correlation algorithm is well suited for the highly parallel architecture of the GPU, resulting in the performance gains we saw in the first example of this chapter. The algorithm for computing the Pearson correlation, on the other hand, suffers when we switch from CPU to GPU suggesting that it is not suited for the GPU's architecture. It is difficult to pinpoint exactly the reason for the differences in performance between the two algorithms without studying the details of the underlying CUDA code and the GPU's architecture. Before deciding to use GPUs for a specific task, it is best to benchmark the relative performance of GPUs versus CPUs, as we have done here:

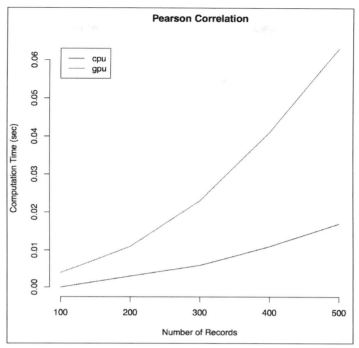

Computation times of calculating Pearson correlations in GPU versus CPU

In general, these factors can affect the GPU's performance:

- GPUs work best for data parallel problems (see *Chapter 8, Multiplying Performance with Parallel Computing* for a definition of data parallelism). They are not suited for tasks that require large amounts of synchronization between threads.

- GPU's performance depends on the amount of data transferred between the main memory (RAM) and the GPU's memory, because the connection between the RAM and GPU's memory has a low bandwidth. Good GPU programming should minimize this data transfer.

Addressing these factors requires programming in the low-level GPU interfaces provided by RCUDA or OpenCL. Other efforts are being made to minimize the efforts required by programmers to optimize a CUDA or OpenCL code. For example, to address the RAM-GPU memory bottleneck, AMD has released a GPU that combines the RAM and GPU memories in a single card.

Summary

In this chapter, we learned how to speed certain computations in R by leveraging GPUs. Given that most computers today come with a GPU, this gives a quick opportunity to improve the performance of R programs. This is especially true with the growing number of packages that interface R with GPUs. Some, such as gputools, require no knowledge of CUDA or OpenCL at all. GPUs do not guarantee improved performance for all tasks.

In the next chapter, we will turn our attention to address RAM-related issues in R programs.

6
Simple Tweaks to Use Less RAM

So far, we have learned the techniques to overcome CPU limitations and improve the speed of R programs. As you can recall from *Chapter 1, Understanding R's Performance – Why Are R Programs Sometimes Slow?* that another key constraint of R is memory. All the data that an R program needs to perform its tasks on must be loaded into the computer's memory or RAM. RAM is also needed for any intermediate computations, so the amount of RAM needed to process a given dataset can be many times the size of the dataset, depending on the type of tasks or algorithms being executed. This can become a problem when a large dataset needs to be processed, or when there is little RAM available to complete the tasks.

In this chapter and the next, we will learn how to optimize the RAM utilization of R programs so that memory-intensive tasks can be executed successfully.

This chapter covers:

- Reusing objects without taking up more memory
- Removing intermediate data when it is no longer needed
- Calculating values on the fly instead of storing them persistently
- Swapping active and nonactive data

Reusing objects without taking up more memory

The first tweak takes advantage of how R manages the memory of objects using a **copy-on-modification** model. In this model, when a copy of an object x is made, for example with y <- x, it is not actually copied in the memory. Rather, the new variable y simply points to the same block of memory that contains x. The first time when y is modified, R copies the data into a new block of memory so that x and y have their own copies of the data. That is why this model of memory management is called copy-on-modification. What this means is that new objects can sometimes be created from existing objects without taking up additional memory. To identify potential memory bottlenecks and manage the memory utilization of R programs, it is helpful to understand when R copies data and when it does not.

Take for example the following code, which generates a numeric vector x with 1 million elements and creates a list y that contains two copies of x. We can examine the size of the objects using the object.size() function:

```
x <- runif(1e6)
print(object.size(x), units = "auto")
## 7.6 Mb
y <- list(x, x)
print(object.size(y), units = "auto")
## 15.3 Mb
```

At first glance, it looks like there are two objects: x, which takes up 7.6 MB of the memory, and y, which takes up 15.3 MB. However, the memory utilization can be measured in a different way, and with surprising results:

```
library(pryr)
object_size(x)
## 8 MB
object_size(y)
## 8 MB
```

The object_size() function from the CRAN package pryr measures the sizes of x and y slightly differently and more accurately than object.size() from the base R. It reports that y, which contains two numeric vectors takes up only 8 MB—the same as x, which is a single numeric vector of the same length. How can that be? The address() function from the pryr package reveals the actual blocks of memory that each object points to:

```
address(x)
## [1] "0x10f992000"
```

```
address(y)
## [1] "0x7ff18b30e478"
address(y[[1]])
## [1] "0x10f992000"
address(y[[2]])
## [1] "0x10f992000"
```

As expected, y, a list, points to a different memory location than x, a numeric vector, indicating that it is a different object. But the two elements of y point to the original object x in the memory. R is smart about not copying objects unnecessarily. In this case, it simply created two pointers in y that point to x. This is so efficient that in fact, x and y combined together take up only 8 MB, which is the size of x!

```
object_size(x, y)
## 8 MB
```

 Actually, a tiny bit of extra memory is needed to store y and its pointers to x, but that is negligible and does not show up in this measurement.

When one of the vectors in y is modified, R creates a new copy, since this vector is now different from x:

```
y[[1]][1] <- 0
address(x)
## [1] "0x10f992000"
address(y[[1]])
## [1] "0x110134000"
address(y[[2]])
## [1] "0x10f992000"
object_size(y)
## 16 MB
object_size(x, y)
## 16 MB
```

The y[[1]] vector now points to a different vector in the memory than x and y[[2]]. As a result, y takes up 16 MB of RAM while x and y combined still take up only 16 MB (since y[[2]] still points to x). Another way to track this is when an object is copied to use tracemem(), which gives an alert whenever the object being tracked is copied. See what happens to y[[2]] when it is modified:

```
tracemem(y[[2]])
## [1] "<0x10f992000>"
y[[2]][1] <- 0
## tracemem[0x10f992000 -> 0x1108d6000]:
untracemem(y[[2]])
```

The `tracemem[0x10f992000 -> 0x1108d6000]` line indicates that a copy of vector `y[[2]]` was made when it was modified and gives the memory address of the new copy. Now, `x`, `y[[1]]`, and `y[[2]]` are different objects in memory, hence the total memory used by `x` and `y` is 24 MB:

```
address(x)
## [1] "0x10f992000"
address(y[[1]])
## [1] "0x110134000"
address(y[[2]])
## [1] "0x1108d6000"
object_size(y)
## 16 MB
object_size(x, y)
## 24 MB
```

When an element of `y` is modified, a copy of `x` needs to be made so that the original object `x` is unmodified. Otherwise, modifying one object will cause unintended modifications to the other, resulting in errors in the program that might be difficult to find.

The way in which R determines whether an object should be copied is by tracking whether other objects refer to it. When `y` was created, R knew that `x` is being used elsewhere and a copy needs to be made when it is modified.

 R counts only up to two references, which is sufficient for it to determine whether to copy an object or not. As long as two or more variables refer to the same object, R will make a copy of it when it is modified.

Now, when we modify `x` for the first time, R makes a copy of it because `x` had been referred to by `y` before. Even though `y` now has its own copies of the data, R errs on the side of caution and makes a copy of `x` to avoid potential conflicts. Subsequent modifications to `x`, however, do not lead to unnecessary copying, as the new copy of `x` is not being used anywhere else, as this example shows:

```
tracemem(x)
## [1] "<0x10f992000>"
x[1]<- 1
## tracemem[0x10f992000 -> 0x111078000]:
```

```
x[1]<- 1
x[1]<- 0.5
x[2] <- 0.3
untracemem(x)
```

In general, as long as a vector has not been referred to by any other object, R allows it to be modified in place, avoiding the CPU and RAM overheads to make copies of the vector.

> This example does not work in RStudio:
> ```
> tracemem(x)
> ## [1] "<0x10e73c000>"
> x[1] <- 0
> ## tracemem[0x10e73c000 -> 0x110d66000]:
> x[2] <- 1
> ## tracemem[0x110d66000 -> 0x115478000]:
> x[3] <- 0.5
> ## tracemem[0x115478000 -> 0x115c79000]:
> untracemem(x)
> ```
> This is because RStudio keeps a reference of every object in its own environment, so R thinks that x is being referred to elsewhere. It creates a copy of x every time it is modified, to be safe.

Now that we understand when R copies data, we can optimize R programs in order to avoid copying the data unnecessarily. For example, say we have two vectors containing the ages and genders of 1 million customers:

```
customer.age <- sample(18:100, 1e6, replace=TRUE)
customer.gender <- sample(c("Male", "Female"), 1e6, TRUE)
```

The retailer uses "cust #" for customer IDs. We want to label each vector with the customer IDs so that we can easily look up the information by the customer ID, using expressions like customer.age["cust 1"]. One way to do this is to separately construct the names for each vector. The two vectors combined will then take up 84 MB of memory:

```
names(customer.age) <- paste("cust", 1:1e6)
names(customer.gender) <- paste("cust", 1:1e6)
object_size(customer.age, customer.gender)
## 84 MB
```

Alternatively, the names can be stored in a separate vector that the age and gender vectors then can refer to:

```
customer.names <- paste("cust", 1:1e6)
names(customer.age) <- customer.names
names(customer.gender) <- customer.names
object_size(customer.age, customer.gender, customer.names)
## 76 MB
```

This simple change resulted in a saving of 8 MB of memory. On larger, more complex data structures, these savings from not copying data unnecessarily can be significant.

The same copy-on-modification behavior applies to function arguments. When an object is passed to a function, it is not copied; R simply provides a pointer to the object. If, however, the object is modified within the function, R creates a copy of that object in the function's environment so that the original object is not modified in any way outside the function. In programming language parlance, this is called **pass by value** because functions are given the value of their arguments. This is part of R's design as a *functional programming language*. Contrast this with **pass by reference**, which is sometimes used in other programming languages, such as Java and C/C++, where functions can be given references or pointers to the memory's addresses. In this case, functions can modify their arguments without creating additional copies in memory, and the modifications persist even after the functions exit.

A consequence of R's pass by value model for functions means that many functions need to make a copy of the data they are given. For example, calling sort(x) returns a new vector with the sorted values of x, rather than sorting the values in place (which is often the practice in Java and C/C++). Calling functions like sort() often requires additional free memory that is at least as large as the original data and sometimes more.

Removing intermediate data when it is no longer needed

In large R programs, objects are created in many places. Often, an object that is created in an earlier part of the program is not needed in later parts of the program. When faced with memory limits, it is useful to free up memory taken up by objects when they are no longer needed, so that subsequent parts of the program can run successfully.

The main tool for this is the `rm()` function that removes a given list of objects from the current R environment.

In the following example, we have a data frame containing 500,000 transactions from a retail store and the items within each transaction. Each row of the data frame represents a unique transaction-item pair that occurred in a sales database. Although, we have to generate the data for this example in a real business context, this data could be extracted from a retailer's sales database:

```
trans.lengths <- rpois(5e5, 3) + 1L
trans <- rep.int(1:5e5, trans.lengths)
items <- unlist(lapply(trans.lengths, sample.int, n = 1000))
sales.data <- data.frame(trans = trans, item = items)
```

The data looks like this where, for example, the first nine rows indicate that transaction 1 includes items 680, 846, 196, and so on (the data that you generate might look different):

```
head(sales.data, 15)
##    trans item
## 1      1  680
## 2      1  846
## 3      1  196
## 4      1  191
## 5      1   20
## 6      1  852
## 7      1  623
## 8      1  206
## 9      1  775
## 10     2  624
## 11     2   31
## 12     2  718
## 13     2  190
## 14     3  482
## 15     3  946
```

Our task is to find common baskets of items, that is, items that appear frequently together in the same transactions, or frequent itemsets. The `apriori()` function in the `arules` CRAN package can be used to find these frequent itemsets. But it does not accept data in the form of transaction-item pairs that we can extract from a sales database. Instead, `arules` defines the `transactions` class that it accepts as input. We need to split the items column of the data frame into the different transactions and then coerce the resulting list into a `transactions` object:

```
library(arules)
```

```
trans.list <- split(sales.data$item, sales.data$trans)
trans.arules <- as(trans.list, "transactions")
```

We can now call the `apriori()` function to find the frequent itemsets. In this example, we want itemsets that have a support of at least 0.3, that is, sets of items that appear in at least 30 percent of the transactions.

```
freq.itemsets <- apriori(trans.arules, list(support = 0.3))
```

When we started with the data frame of transaction-item pairs, we had to convert it into a few different formats before the data could be used by `apriori()`. Each of these intermediate data structures takes up valuable memory:

```
object_size(sales.data)
## 16 MB
object_size(trans.list)
## 62.1 MB
object_size(trans.arules)
## 44 MB
```

When the dataset is large or when memory is scarce, `apriori()` might fail to execute as it runs out of memory. In such situations, `rm()` can be used to free up memory by deleting unneeded objects before calling `apriori()` or even between each data transformation step. The following code illustrates this:

```
trans.list <- split(sales.data$item, sales.data$trans)
rm(sales.data)
trans.arules <- as(trans.list, "transactions")
rm(trans.list)
freq.itemsets <- apriori(trans.arules, list(support = 0.3))
```

Another technique to automatically remove temporary variables is to encapsulate code in functions. This way, any variables created in the function will automatically be deleted when the function exists. For example, say we only need to remove temporary variables before calling `apriori()`, because that is when the code tends to run into memory limits. We can encapsulate all the previous lines of codes in a function:

```
# Automatically remove temporary variables by encapsulating code
# in a function
prepare_data <- function(sales.data) {
    trans.list <- split(sales.data$item, sales.data$trans)
```

```
            trans.arules <- as(trans.list, "transactions")
            return(trans.arules)
}
trans.arules <- prepare_data(sales.data)
freq.itemsets <- apriori(trans.arules, list(support = 0.3))
```

After calling `prepare_data()`, any temporary variables created within it are deleted without having to explicitly call `rm()`. In this case, only one temporary variable, `trans.list` is deleted. But the same technique can be used when more temporary variables are declared in the function. Not only is this means of removing temporary variables convenient, it also makes the code more readable and easier to maintain.

In large R programs, periodic removal of large data structures can help to minimize overall memory usage. When `rm()` is called, the memory might not be freed and returned to the operating system immediately. Rather, R's **garbage collector** automatically frees the memory when it is needed, or when the amount of memory from removed objects exceeds a threshold.

Calculating values on the fly instead of storing them persistently

While executing an R program, it is sometimes convenient to cache all the data needed by the program, including the results of intermediate computations into a RAM prior to execution. During the execution, as and when the program needs to access any part of the data, it can be done very rapidly as all the data has been loaded into the R workspace. Caching intermediate results in RAM can save computational time significantly, especially when they are accessed frequently, as unnecessary recalculation of the data is avoided.

This is not a problem when the cached data can fit into RAM. However, it becomes a problem when there is not enough memory space to contain the data. The good news is, in many cases, the program does not need all parts of the data at the same time. One solution is to swap in and out portions of the data between RAM and the hard disk. Because disk I/O is slow, as we have established in *Chapter 1, Understanding R's Performance – Why Are R Programs Sometimes Slow?*, this approach might result in a slow execution. A better solution is to calculate and recalculate portions of the data that are needed at the moment. Yes, calculation costs computational time, but it is often less costly than disk I/O.

Let's look at an example from a common task in data science: hierarchical clustering. In some commonly used variants of hierarchical clustering, such as the single, complete, and average linkage, one important step in the algorithm is to calculate the distance matrix between every pair of observations in the dataset, and then decide which pair of observations is the closest to each other. This step can be accomplished by the following code, in which we have artificially created a random dataset A, with 10,000 observations (rows) and 10 features (columns). The code first calculates the distance matrix of A, sets the diagonal element of the distance matrix to NA because an observation is always closest to itself and finally finds the closest pair using the which() function. In this instance, observations 6778 and 6737 are found to be the closest pair. To execute this program, about 801 MB of RAM is required, as can be seen from the outputs of object_size() in the following code. This is because even though the dataset only occupies 800 KB, its distance matrix needs about a quadratic amount of the original space because it is storing all the pairwise distances:

```
A <- matrix(rnorm(1E5), 1E4, 10)
dist_mat <- as.matrix(dist(A))
diag(dist_mat) <- NA
res1 <- which(dist_mat == min(dist_mat, na.rm=T), arr.ind = T)[1,]
res1
##   row   col
## 6778 6737
object_size(A)
## 800 kB
object_size(dist_mat)
## 801 MB
```

On close inspection, we do not actually need the whole distance matrix at once to find the closest pair. It is possible to calculate the set of pairwise distances between the first observation and the rest of the observations to get the minimum pair for this set; repeat the process for the second observation and then compare the minimum of the two sets and so on. Doing this incurs additional steps and hence longer computational time, but it demands only a small fraction of RAM compared to that of the preceding code (because only a chunk of the distance matrix is maintained at a given time). The code to do this is shown below. It first calculates the distances between all the observations in A with the observation 1 in A (using the pdist package) and then finds and saves the closest pair only for this chunk to a temporary list output. This process is repeated for the observations 2, 3, …, 10,000 in A using lapply. The set of closest pairs from every chunk is stored in the temp_res list. The final step is to find the minimum pair among this set and store it in the variable res2. Evaluating the output of res2 reveals the same result as the one found using the preceding code. However, this time we need only 2.7 MB of memory for the temp_res list.

```
library(pdist)
```

```
temp_res <- lapply(1:nrow(A), function(x) {
  temp <- as.matrix(pdist(X = A, Y = A[x,]));
  temp[x] <- NA;
  output_val <- min(temp, na.rm=T);
  output_ind <- c(x, which(temp == output_val));
  output <- list(val = output_val, ind = output_ind);
})
val_vec <- sapply(temp_res, FUN=function(x) x$val)
ind_vec <- sapply(temp_res, FUN=function(x) x$ind)
res2 <- ind_vec[, which.min(val_vec)]
res2
## [1] 6778 6737
object_size(temp_res)
## 2.72 MB
object_size(val_vec)
## 80 kB
object_size(ind_vec)
## 80.2 kB
```

Indeed the time needed by the second approach is longer. We can speed this up by parallelizing the code, for example by substituting `lapply()` with `parLApply()` of the `parallel` package (see *Chapter 8, Multiplying Performance with Parallel Computing*). In practice, for a specific case of finding the closest pair of observations efficiently without storing a full distance matrix, we can leverage optimized k-nearest neighbor functions, like the `knn()` function in the FNN package. Where such an alternative optimized package is unavailable, the approach of calculating values on the fly as illustrated in the preceding code is useful to reduce memory use.

Swapping active and nonactive data

In some situations, large objects that are removed to free up memory are needed later in the program. R provides tools to save data to the disk and reload them later when enough memory is available. Returning to the retail sales data example, suppose that we need the `sales.data` data frame for further processing after mining for frequent itemsets. We can save it to the disk using `saveRDS()` and reload it later using `readRDS()`:

```
trans.list <- split(sales.data$item, sales.data$trans)
saveRDS(sales.data, "sales.data.rds")
rm(sales.data)
trans.arules <- as(trans.list, "transactions")
rm(trans.list)
freq.itemsets <- apriori(trans.arules, list(support = 0.3))
sales.data <- readRDS("sales.data.rds")
# Perform further processing with sales.data
```

The `saveRDS()` and `readRDS()` functions save one object at a time without the name of the object. For example, the name `sales.data` is not saved. However, the column names `trans` and `items` are saved. As an alternative, the `save()` and `load()` functions can be used to handle multiple objects or even all objects in an environment, along with their variable names.

Summary

In this chapter, we learned about the copy-on-modification semantics of R's memory management. A good understanding of how this works enables us to find opportunities to reduce the memory consumption of R programs.

We also saw how temporary variables and intermediate computations can be removed from the environment when they are no longer needed, to free up memory for subsequent computations. Besides removing temporary variables explicitly, we learned two other ways to manage temporary variables automatically. First, on the fly computations produce intermediate data without creating variables that persist in the memory. Second, functions are a useful way to group related operations and automatically remove temporary variables when exiting the functions.

Finally, we saw how to save data to the disk to free up memory and reload them later when needed.

In the next chapter, we will explore more advanced techniques in order to optimize memory consumption and allow R programs to work with larger datasets, even data that is too big to fit in the memory.

7
Processing Large Datasets with Limited RAM

In the previous chapter, we learned how to optimize the memory consumption of R programs by reducing the copying of data and by removing temporary data. Sometimes, that is still not enough. We might have data that is too large to even fit into memory, let alone perform any computations on them, or even if the data can fit into memory, there is not much free memory left for the analyses that we need to perform.

In this chapter, we will learn advanced techniques to overcome memory limitations and process large datasets.

This chapter covers:

- Using memory-efficient data structures
- Using memory-mapped files and processing data in chunks

Using memory-efficient data structures

One of the first things to consider when you work with a large dataset is whether the same information can be stored and processed using more memory-efficient data structures. But first we need to know how data is stored in R. Vectors are the basic building blocks of almost all data types in R. R provides atomic vectors of logical, integer, numeric, complex, character and raw types. Many other data structures are also built from vectors. Lists, for example, are essentially vectors in R's internal storage structures. They differ from atomic vectors in the way that they store pointers to other R objects rather than atomic values. That is why lists can contain objects of different types.

t's examine how much memory is required for each of the atomic data types.

do that, we will create vectors of each type with 1 million elements and measure their memory consumption using `object.size()` (for character vectors, we will call `rep.int(NA_character_, 1e6)`, which will create a truly empty character vector containing the NA values, which as we shall see shortly, takes up less memory than a character vector containing empty strings):

```
object.size(logical(1e6))
## 4000040 bytes
object.size(integer(1e6))
## 4000040 bytes
object.size(numeric(1e6))
## 8000040 bytes
object.size(complex(1e6))
## 16000040 bytes
object.size(rep.int(NA_character_, 1e6))
## 8000040 bytes
object.size(raw(1e6))
## 1000040 bytes
object.size(vector("list", 1e6))
## 8000040 bytes
```

These results were taken from a 64-bit version of R. Notice that all these vectors take up memory in multiples of 1 million plus an extra 40 bytes. These 40 bytes are taken up by the headers of the vectors that R uses to store information about the vectors, such as the lengths and data types. The remaining space is taken up by the data stored in the vectors.

By dividing these numbers by 1 million, we see that raw values take up 1 byte each, logical and integer values 4 bytes, numeric values 8 bytes, and complex values 16 bytes. The following figure depicts the structure and memory required for these types of vectors:

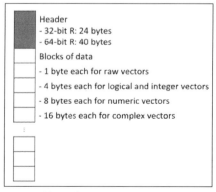

Internal structure of logical, integer, numeric, and complex vectors

Character vectors and lists are a little different because they do not store the actual data within their vectors. Instead, they store pointers to other vectors that contain the actual data. In the computer's memory, each element of a character vector or list is a pointer that occupies 4 bytes in a 32-bit R and 8 bytes in a 64-bit R. This is depicted in the following figure:

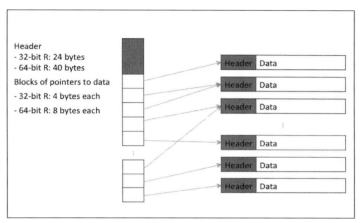

Internal structure of lists and character vectors

Let's examine character vectors more closely to see how they are stored. To do this, we will generate three different character vectors, all having 1 million strings with 10 characters each. The first vector simply contains 1 million copies of the "0123456789" string, generated using the formatC() function to take up ten characters. The second vector contains 1,000 copies of 1,000 unique strings, generated using formatC() to take up 10 characters. The third vector contains 1 million unique strings with 10 characters each. Because these vectors contain the same number of strings with the same length, we would expect them to take up the same amount of memory. Let's test this hypothesis:

```
object.size(rep.int("0123456789", 1e6))
## 8000096 bytes
object.size(rep.int(formatC(seq_len(1e3), width = 10), 1e3))
## 8056040 bytes
object.size(formatC(seq_len(1e6), width = 10))
## 64000040 bytes
```

It turns out that the three character vectors take up vastly different amounts of memory, depending on the actual content of the strings. This is because R stores only one copy of each unique string in its CHARSXP cache in order to save memory. The character vectors that we created actually store pointers to the strings in this cache, rather than the strings themselves.

Furthermore, each of the strings in this cache is a full-fledged R vector with a 24- or 40-byte header (in a 32-bit and 64-bit R respectively) and exactly one string. The null character is appended to the end of the string, and the total vector length is rounded up to the nearest multiple of eight. So, for example, the string `0123456789` would be stored as `0123456789\0` (where `\0` is the null character) plus five more bytes to make a total of 16 bytes. Adding on the 40-byte header in a 64-bit R, this 10-character string occupies 56 bytes of memory.

Turning back to the results, the first vector with 1 million copies of `0123456789` requires 8,000,040 bytes for the character vector itself that contains pointers and another 56 bytes for storing the string itself. This makes for a total of 8,000,096 bytes, as reported by `object.size()`.

The second vector contains 1,000 unique strings, so it uses a total of *8,000,040 + 1,000 × 56 = 8,056,040* bytes of memory.

The third vector contains 1 million unique strings, so it uses a total of *8,000,040 + 1,000,000 × 56 = 64,000,040* bytes of memory.

Evidently the memory consumption of character vectors depends on the number of unique strings contained in the vector.

Smaller data types

Having understood how atomic vectors are stored in R, we now look at some simple strategies to reduce the memory footprint of large datasets so that they might fit in memory for analysis.

One way is to coerce data to smaller data types, where possible. For example, if a dataset contains only integer values, storing them in an integer instead of numeric vector reduces memory consumption by about half:

```
object.size(as.numeric(seq_len(1e6)))
## 8000040 bytes
object.size(as.integer(seq_len(1e6)))
## 4000040 bytes
```

This also applies to character strings. Where there are many duplicated strings in a character vector, converting it to a factor vector can reduce the memory consumption, since factors are actually integer vectors that index a character vector of the unique strings (the levels of the factor) that appear in the data:

```
strings <- rep.int(formatC(seq_len(1e4), width = 1000), 100)
```

```
factors <- factor(strings)
object.size(strings)
## 18480040 bytes
object.size(factors)
## 14560400 bytes
```

These same techniques can be applied to the components of other data structures, such as matrices, data frames, and lists that are built on atomic vectors.

Sparse matrices

Sometimes the data might be very sparse, that is, it contains a lot of zeroes or empty values. Instead of storing a full vector of matrix in memory, using *sparse matrices* can significantly reduce the amount of memory required to represent the data. Sparse matrices are provided by the `Matrix` package that comes with R.

Say we have a 1,000 by 1,000 matrix of numbers (1 million elements in total) with about 70 percent zeroes. We can use the `Matrix()` function to create either dense or sparse matrices from this data, depending on the sparse argument:

```
library(Matrix)
n <- rnorm(1e6)
n[sample.int(1e6, 7e5)] <- 0
m.dense <- Matrix(n, 1e3, 1e3, sparse = FALSE)
m.sparse <- Matrix(n, 1e3, 1e3, sparse = TRUE)
object.size(n)
## 8000040 bytes
object.size(m.dense)
## 8001112 bytes
object.size(m.sparse)
## 3605424 bytes
```

The dense matrix requires about the same amount of memory as the numeric vector of raw data. The sparse matrix reduces the size of the data by 55 percent.

Sparse matrices are also very useful for binary data (TRUE/FALSE, 0/1, "yes"/"no", "hot"/"cold", and so on). Simply convert the binary data into logical values, where the majority class is FALSE (if the majority class if TRUE, just invert the data). We can then create sparse matrices that only store information about where the TRUE values occur in the matrix. Again, let's test this on a 70 percent sparse matrix of 1 million logical values:

```
l <- sample(c(FALSE, TRUE), 1e6, TRUE, c(0.7, 0.3))
```

```
m2.dense <- Matrix(1, 1e3, 1e3, sparse = FALSE)
m2.sparse <- Matrix(1, 1e3, 1e3, sparse = TRUE)
object.size(1)
## 4000040 bytes
object.size(m2.dense)
## 4001112 bytes
object.size(m2.sparse)
## 2404384 bytes
```

The sparse logical matrix is even more compact than the sparse numeric matrix, being 33 percent smaller.

Symmetric matrices

Symmetric matrices, that is, matrices that are equal to their transpose are used in many statistical methods. Some examples include distance matrices, correlation matrices, and graph adjacency matrices. It is possible to save memory by keeping only half of the matrix, including the diagonal, since we can generate the other half of the matrix by taking the mirror image of the half matrix. The Matrix package provides the dspMatrix class to efficiently store symmetric matrices:

```
library(Matrix)
data <- matrix(rnorm(1E5), 1E2, 1E3)
A <- cor(data)
isSymmetric(A)
## [1] TRUE
B <- as(A, "dspMatrix")
object.size(A)
## 8000200 bytes
object.size(B)
## 4005320 bytes
```

Beyond sparse and symmetric matrices, the Matrix package provides several other efficient matrix-type data structures including triangular matrices and diagonal matrices. Depending on the type of data, some of these data structures might be even more memory-efficient than the generic sparse or symmetric matrices used in the preceding examples. Furthermore, the package makes it such that basic matrix operations, such as matrix multiplication (%*%), are applicable for both dense and sparse matrices. Hence, in most cases, we do not need to manually port matrix operations from their dense to sparse versions. Consult the documentation of the Matrix package for more details.

Bit vectors

Binary data can be represented in an even more efficient way, using bit vectors. Unlike logical values in R that take up four bytes or 32 bits, bit vectors store each logical value using only one bit. This reduces the memory consumption of logical values by a factor of 32. Bit vectors, however, cannot store the NA value, so they are not suitable for data that contains the NA values.

In R, bit vectors are provided by the `bit` package on CRAN. Let's compare the sizes of a logical vector and the equivalent bit vector:

```
library(bit)
l <- sample(c(TRUE, FALSE), 1e6, TRUE)
b <- as.bit(l)
object.size(l)
## 4000040 bytes
object.size(b)
## 126344 bytes
```

As expected, the bit vector is 3.2 percent, or 1/32 as large as the logical vector.

Bit vectors also allow for much quicker logical operations:

```
library(microbenchmark)
l2 <- sample(c(TRUE, FALSE), 1e6, TRUE)
b2 <- as.bit(l2)
microbenchmark(!l, !b)
## Unit: microseconds
##   expr      min        lq    median        uq       max neval
##     !l 1201.993 1452.2925  1566.966 2951.0405 23045.003   100
##     !b   51.145   64.7185   107.065  113.2045   461.624   100
microbenchmark(l & l2, b & b2)
## Unit: microseconds
##    expr       min        lq     median        uq      max neval
##  l & l2 22808.696 23104.647 23309.7475 24473.137 38334.65   100
##  b & b2    60.948    64.615    78.5025   135.126 13732.20   100
microbenchmark(l == l2, b == b2)
## Unit: microseconds
##     expr      min        lq    median        uq      max neval
##  l == l2 1954.402 2208.3235 2227.8980 2320.104 16825.13   100
##  b == b2   60.263   63.2235   87.7245  121.448 14184.91   100
```

When dealing with large amounts of logical or binary data, bit vectors not only save memory but also provide a speed boost when they are operated on.

Using memory-mapped files and processing data in chunks

Some datasets are so large that even after applying all memory optimization techniques and using the most efficient data types possible, they are still too large to fit in or be processed in the memory. Short of getting additional RAM, one way to work with such large data is to store them on a disk in the form of **memory-mapped files** and load the data into the memory for processing one small chunk at a time.

For example, say we have a dataset that would require 100 GB of RAM if it is fully loaded into the memory and another 100 GB of free memory for the computations that need to be performed on the data. If the computer on which the data is to be processed only has 64 GB of RAM, we might divide the data into four chunks of 25 GB each. The R program will then load the data into the memory one chunk at a time and perform the necessary computations on each chunk. After all the chunks have been processed, the results from each chunk-wise computation will finally be combined in order to compute the final results. Whether this can be done easily depends on the nature of the algorithm that is being run on the data. Some algorithms can easily be converted to compute on chunks of data, while others might require substantial effort to do so.

There are two CRAN packages that provide memory-mapped files to work with large datasets in this manner: bigmemory and ff. We will look at each of these in turn.

The bigmemory package

The bigmemory CRAN package provides a matrix-like data structure called big.matrix. Data stored in big.matrix objects can be of type double (8 bytes, the default), integer (4 bytes), short (2 bytes), or char (1 byte).The big.matrix objects can exist in RAM or in the form of memory-mapped files, and they can be manipulated in very much the same way as standard R matrices.

> At the time of writing, bigmemory is not supported on Windows, but the package authors are working to fix this.

To create a big.matrix object, we can either call big.matrix() to create a new object, or as.big.matrix() to coerce a matrix into big.matrix. For the next example, we will create a new big.matrix object with 1 billion rows and 3 columns in R's temporary folder:

```
library(bigmemory)
```

```
bm <- big.matrix(1e9, 3, backingfile = "bm",
                 backingpath = tempdir())
bm
## An object of class "big.matrix"
## Slot "address":
## <pointer: 0x7fac1950a4a0>
```

Running this might take a while, but when it is done, we have a new object `bm` that stores a pointer to the new memory-mapped file. We can find the new file called `bm` in the temporary directory with a size of 22 GB:

```
aloysius@localhost RtmpG0CQdS $ ls -lh
total 46875024
-rw-r--r--  1 aloysius  staff     22G Sep 18 08:02 bm
-rw-r--r--  1 aloysius  staff    452B Sep 18 08:02 bm.desc
```

Such a large dataset would not have fit into the main memory of most computers. Another file, `bm.desc`, was created alongside the data file. This is used to retrieve the memory-mapped file at a later time or by another R program by calling something like `my.bm <- attach.big.matrix(file.path(tempdir(), "bm.desc"))`.

The `big.matrix` objects support many of the same operations as standard R matrices:

```
typeof(bm)
## [1] "double"
dim(bm)
## [1] 1e+09 3e+00
nrow(bm)
## [1] 1e+09
ncol(bm)
## [1] 3
length(bm)
## [1] 3e+09
bm[1:5, ]
##      [,1] [,2] [,3]
## [1,]    1    0    0
## [2,]    0    1    0
## [3,]    0    0    1
## [4,]    0    0    0
## [5,]    0    0    0
bm[1:3, ] <- diag(3)
bm[1:5, ]
##      [,1] [,2] [,3]
## [1,]    1    0    0
```

```
## [2,]     0     1     0
## [3,]     0     0     1
## [4,]     0     0     0
## [5,]     0     0     0
```

When the subsetting operator [is used, bigmemory materializes the selected portion of the data into the RAM as a matrix. As different parts of a big.matrix are used, bigmemory automatically loads the relevant portions of the data into the RAM and removes portions that are no longer needed. Because everything selected by [is loaded into the memory, care must be taken to ensure that the selected data can fit into the available memory. Calls such as bm[,] will likely lead to out of memory errors.

Let's now see how an R program might work with big.matrix by processing one chunk of it at a time. First we will fill it with random data, one chunk at a time. The first column will contain integers from the Poisson distribution with a mean of 1,000. The second column will contain binary data represented by ones and zeroes. The third will contain real numbers uniformly distributed between 0 and 100,000. The following code fills in bm with these random numbers in 100 chunks of 10 million rows at a time:

```
chunksize <- 1e7
start <- 1
while (start <= nrow(bm)) {
    end <- min(start + chunksize - 1, nrow(bm))
    chunksize <- end - start + 1
    bm[start:end, 1] <- rpois(chunksize, 1e3)
    bm[start:end, 2] <- sample(0:1, chunksize, TRUE,
                               c(0.7, 0.3))
    bm[start:end, 3] <- runif(chunksize, 0, 1e5)
    start <- start + chunksize
}
```

Another example of a chunked computation is to find the standard deviation of each column. Calling sd(bm[1,]) might not work, as even a single column of data can exceed available memory. Two passes through the data are needed: one to compute the mean of each column, and another to compute the squared deviations from the mean.

The data can be split into chunks of 10 million rows, as before. In the first pass, the column means are computed:

```
col.sums <- numeric(3)
chunksize <- 1e7
start <- 1
while (start <= nrow(bm)) {
    end <- min(start + chunksize - 1, nrow(bm))
```

```
        col.sums <- col.sums + colSums(bm[start:end, ])
        start <- start + chunksize
}
col.means <- col.sums / nrow(bm)
```

The code iterates through each chunk of data and computes the column sums of each chunk using the `colSums()` function. This is added to the global column sums, stored in `col.sums`. Once all the chunks have been processed, the column means are computed by dividing `col.sums` by the number of rows in the data.

In the second pass, the squared deviations of the observations from the column means are computed:

```
col.sq.dev <- numeric(3)
start <- 1
while (start <= nrow(bm)) {
    end <- min(start + chunksize - 1, nrow(bm))
    col.sq.dev <- col.sq.dev +
        rowSums((t(bm[start:end, ]) - col.means) ^ 2)
    start <- start + chunksize
}
col.var <- col.sq.dev / (nrow(bm) - 1)
col.sd <- sqrt(col.var)
```

Each chunk of data is first transposed using `t()` so that `col.means` can be subtracted from each column of the transposed data to calculate the deviations from the means. The deviations are then squared and summed over the rows as the data was transposed.

Once all the chunks have been processed, the total squared deviations of each column are then divided by *n-1* to compute the variance of each column. Finally, the square roots of the column variances give the column standard deviations.

The authors of `bigmemory` also wrote a companion package `biganalytics` that provides common statistical functions for `big.matrix` objects. We can compare the results of the preceding exercise with the `colsd()` function from `biganalytics`:

```
library(biganalytics)
col.sd
## [1] 3.162261e+01 4.582687e-01 2.886805e+04
big.col.sd <- colsd(bm)
all.equal(col.sd, big.col.sd)
## [1] TRUE
```

We have seen how to perform computations over chunks of data using `big.matrix` objects. The authors of `bigmemory` have also created other CRAN packages that provide useful functions that operate over `big.matrix` objects. These are listed in the following table:

Package	Samples of functions provided
biganalytics	Statistics: `colmean()`, `colmin()`, `min()`, `colmax()`, `max()`, `colrange()`, `range()`, `colvar()`, `colsd()`, `colsum()`, `sum()`, `colprod()`, `prod()`, and `colna()`
	Apply: `apply()`
	Linear models: `biglm.big.matrix()`, `bigglim.big.matrix()`
	Clustering: `bigkmeans()`
bigtabulate	Table and `tapply`: `bigtabulate()`, `bigtable()`, `bigtsummary()`
	Split: `bigsplit()`
bigalgebra	Arithmetic operations

The ff package

While `big.matrix` is useful for data that can be coerced to the same type, sometimes a more data frame-like memory-mapped format is required while dealing with heterogeneous data types. The `ff` CRAN package provides this capability.

The `ff` CRAN package supports more data types than `bigmemory`. The following table shows the different data types, called `vmodes`, that can be stored in `ff` vectors, arrays and data frames.

Data type or vmode	Description
Boolean	1-bit logical without NA
Logical	2-bit logical with NA
Quad	2-bit unsigned integer without NA
Nibble	4-bit unsigned integer without NA
Byte	8-bit signed integer with NA
Ubyte	8-bit unsigned integer without NA
Short	16-bit signed integer with NA
Ushort	16-bit unsigned integer without NA
Integer	32-bit signed integer with NA
Single	32-bit float
Double	64-bit float

Data type or vmode	Description
`Complex`	2 x 64 bit float
`Raw`	8-bit unsigned char
`Factor`	Factor (stored as `integer`)
`Ordered`	Ordered factor (stored as `integer`)
`POSIXct`	POSIXct (stored as a `double`)
`Date`	Date (stored as `double`)

The `ff` objects can be created by passing a vector of values to the `ff()` function:

```
i <- ff(1:1e6)
i
## ff (open) integer length=1000000 (1000000)
##         [1]       [2]       [3]       [4]       [5]       [6]
##           1         2         3         4         5         6
##         [7]       [8]             [999993] [999994] [999995]
##           7         8         :    999993   999994   999995
##    [999996] [999997] [999998] [999999] [1000000]
##      999996   999997   999998   999999  1000000
filename(i)
## [1] "/private/var/folders/xw/xp2p4mjd3nb6n6h30w67jkdc0000gn/T/
## RtmptxP4qw/ff449847497df9.ff"
```

Because no filename was specified, `ff()` automatically creates a new file in R's temporary directory. The filename can also be specified using the `filename` argument, as shown in the next example.

If a scalar is passed to `ff()` along with the dimensions for the new `ff` object, the scalar value will be used to initialize the object:

```
j <- ff(FALSE, dim = c(50, 100),
        filename = file.path(tempdir(), "j.ff"))
j
## ff (open) logical length=5000 (5000) dim=c(50,100)
## dimorder=c(1,2)
##          [,1]  [,2]  [,3]  [,4]  [,5]  [,6]  [,7]  [,8]  [,100]
## [1,]   FALSE FALSE FALSE FALSE FALSE FALSE FALSE FALSE :  FALSE
## [2,]   FALSE FALSE FALSE FALSE FALSE FALSE FALSE FALSE :  FALSE
## [3,]   FALSE FALSE FALSE FALSE FALSE FALSE FALSE FALSE :  FALSE
## [4,]   FALSE FALSE FALSE FALSE FALSE FALSE FALSE FALSE :  FALSE
## [5,]   FALSE FALSE FALSE FALSE FALSE FALSE FALSE FALSE :  FALSE
## :          :     :     :     :     :     :     :   : :     :
## [46,]  FALSE FALSE FALSE FALSE FALSE FALSE FALSE FALSE :  FALSE
```

```
## [47,] FALSE FALSE FALSE FALSE FALSE FALSE FALSE FALSE : FALSE
## [48,] FALSE FALSE FALSE FALSE FALSE FALSE FALSE FALSE : FALSE
## [49,] FALSE FALSE FALSE FALSE FALSE FALSE FALSE FALSE : FALSE
## [50,] FALSE FALSE FALSE FALSE FALSE FALSE FALSE FALSE : FALSE
```

The vmode argument sets the storage mode of the ff object:

```
q <- ff(sample(0:3, 1e6, TRUE), vmode = "quad")
q
## ff (open) quad length=1000000 (1000000)
##           [1]       [2]       [3]       [4]       [5]       [6]
##             2         2         2         2         0         1
##           [7]       [8]             [999993]  [999994]  [999995]
##             1         0         :         1         0         1
##      [999996]  [999997]  [999998]  [999999] [1000000]
##             0         1         0         0         0
```

Data frames can be constructed using ffdf(). Here, we create a new ffdf object using the integer and quad ff vectors created in the preceding code:

```
d <- ffdf(i, q)
d[1:5, ]
##   i q
## 1 1 2
## 2 2 2
## 3 3 2
## 4 4 2
## 5 5 0
vmode(d)
##         i         q
## "integer"    "quad"
```

The ff objects provide the convenient chunk() function to split up the data into chunks based on the available memory. With its default arguments, chunk() recommends to load the entire data frame d in one chunk:

```
chunk(d)
## [[1]]
## range index (ri) from 1 to 1000000 maxindex 1000000
```

The maximum chunk size in bytes can also be set using the BATCHBYTES argument. When it is set to 2 million bytes, chunk() recommends splitting the data into four chunks:

```
ch <- chunk(d, BATCHBYTES = 2e6)
ch
```

```
## [[1]]
## range index (ri) from 1 to 250000 maxindex 1000000
##
## [[2]]
## range index (ri) from 250001 to 500000 maxindex 1000000
##
## [[3]]
## range index (ri) from 500001 to 750000 maxindex 1000000
##
## [[4]]
## range index (ri) from 750001 to 1000000 maxindex 1000000
```

In general, it is desirable to have smaller number chunks, as every chunk incurs an (typically small) I/O overhead that is required every time an R session needs to read data from disk.

The indices returned by chunk() can be used to index the rows of an ffdf or ff object. The following code iterates through each chunk of data, selecting the chunk with d[idx,] and q[idx], and performs some computations on the chunk.

```
total <- numeric(2)
quad.table <- integer(4)
names(quad.table) <- 0:3
for (idx in ch) {
    total <- total + colSums(d[idx, ])
    quad.table <- quad.table + table(q[idx])
}
total
##              i            q
## 500000500000     1500191
quad.table
##      0      1      2      3
## 249939 249964 250064 250033
```

The ff CRAN package has a companion package, ffbase, that provides useful functions for manipulating ff and ffdf objects. Here is a sample of these functions:

- **Mathematics**: abs(), sign(), sqrt(), ceiling(), floor(), log(), exp(), cos(), cosh(), sin(), sinh(), gamma()

- **Summaries**: all(), any(), max(), min(), cumsum(), cummin()

- **Uniqueness**: duplicated(), unique()

- **Apply**: ffdfdply()

When we are finished with the `ff` or `ffdf` objects, we can delete the files using `delete()` and remove the R variables using `rm()`:

```
delete(d)
## [1] TRUE
delete(lm)
## [1] TRUE
rm(d)
rm(lm)
```

Because the underlying vectors `i` and `q` are also deleted while deleting the data frame `d`, attempting to delete the vectors will result in an error. We can simply remove the R objects:

```
delete(i)
## [1] FALSE
## Warning message:
## In file.remove(attr(physical, "filename")) :
##    cannot remove file '/private/var/folders/xw/
## xp2p4mjd3nb6n6h30w67jkdc0000gn/T/RtmptxP4qw/ff449847497df9.ff',
## reason 'No such file or directory'
rm(i)
rm(q)
```

Summary

In this chapter, we learned how R stores vectors in memory, and how to estimate the amount of memory required for different types of data. We also learned how to use more efficient data structures like sparse matrices and bit vectors in order to store some types of data, so that they can be fully loaded and processed in the memory.

For datasets that are still too large, we used `big.matrix`, `ff`, and `ffdf` objects to store memory on disk using memory-mapped files and processed the data one chunk at a time. The `bigmemory` and `ff` packages, along with their companion packages, provide a rich set of functionality for memory-mapped files that cannot be covered fully, in this book. We encourage you to look up the documentation for these packages to learn more about how to take advantage of the power of memory-mapped files when you handle large datasets.

In the next chapter, we will look beyond running R in a single process or thread, and learn how to run R computations in parallel.

8

Multiplying Performance with Parallel Computing

In this chapter, we will learn how to write and execute a parallel R code, where different parts of the code run simultaneously. So far, we have learned various ways to optimize the performance of R programs running serially, that is in a single process. This does not take full advantage of the computing power of modern CPUs with multiple cores. Parallel computing allows us to tap into all the computational resources available and to speed up the execution of R programs by many times. We will examine the different types of parallelism and how to implement them in R, and we will take a closer look at a few performance considerations when designing the parallel architecture of R programs.

This chapter covers the following topics:

- Data parallelism versus task parallelism
- Implementing data parallel algorithms
- Implementing task parallel algorithms
- Executing tasks in parallel on a cluster of computers
- Shared memory versus distributed memory parallelism
- Optimizing parallel performance

Data parallelism versus task parallelism

Many modern software applications are designed to run computations in parallel in order to take advantage of the multiple CPU cores available on almost any computer today. Many R programs can similarly be written in order to run in parallel. However, the extent of possible parallelism depends on the computing task involved. On one side of the scale are **embarrassingly parallel** tasks, where there are no dependencies between the parallel subtasks; such tasks can be made to run in parallel very easily. An example of this is, building an ensemble of decision trees in a random forest algorithm—randomized decision trees can be built independently from one another and in parallel across tens or hundreds of CPUs, and can be combined to form the random forest. On the other end of the scale are tasks that cannot be parallelized, as each step of the task depends on the results of the previous step. One such example is a depth-first search of a tree, where the subtree to search at each step depends on the path taken in previous steps. Most algorithms fall somewhere in between with some steps that must run serially and some that can run in parallel. With this in mind, careful thought must be given when designing a parallel code that works correctly and efficiently.

Often an R program has some parts that have to be run serially and other parts that can run in parallel. Before making the effort to parallelize any of the R code, it is useful to have an estimate of the potential performance gains that can be achieved. **Amdahl's law** provides a way to estimate the best attainable performance gain when you convert a code from serial to parallel execution. It divides a computing task into its serial and potentially-parallel parts and states that the time needed to execute the task in parallel will be no less than this formula:

$T(n) = T(1)(P + (1-P)/n)$, where:

- $T(n)$ is the time taken to execute the task using n parallel processes
- P is the proportion of the whole task that is strictly serial

The theoretical best possible speed up of the parallel algorithm is thus:

$S(n) = T(1) / T(n) = 1 / (P + (1-P)/n)$

For example, given a task that takes 10 seconds to execute on one processor, where half of the task can be run in parallel, then the best possible time to run it on four processors is $T(4) = 10(0.5 + (1-0.5)/4) = 6.25$ seconds.

The theoretical best possible speed up of the parallel algorithm with four processors is *1 / (0.5 + (1-0.5)/4) = 1.6x.*

The following figure shows you how the theoretical best possible execution time decreases as more CPU cores are added. Notice that the execution time reaches a limit that is just above five seconds. This corresponds to the half of the task that must be run serially, where parallelism does not help.

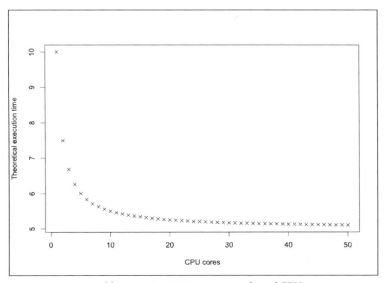

Best possible execution time versus number of CPU cores

In general, Amdahl's law means that the fastest execution time for any parallelized algorithm is limited by the time needed for the serial portions of the algorithm. Bear in mind that Amdahl's law provides only a theoretical estimate. It does not account for the overheads of parallel computing (such as starting and coordinating tasks) and assumes that the parallel portions of the algorithm are infinitely scalable. In practice, these factors might significantly limit the performance gains of parallelism, so use Amdahl's law only to get a rough estimate of the maximum speedup possible.

There are two main classes of parallelism: data parallelism and task parallelism. Understanding these concepts helps to determine what types of tasks can be modified to run in parallel.

In **data parallelism**, a dataset is divided into multiple partitions. Different partitions are distributed to multiple processors, and the same task is executed on each partition of data. Take for example, the task of finding the maximum value in a vector dataset, say one that has one billion numeric data points. A serial algorithm to do this would look like the following code, which iterates over every element of the data in sequence to search for the largest value. (This code is intentionally verbose to illustrate how the algorithm works; in practice, the max() function in R, though also serial in nature, is much faster.)

```
serialmax <- function(data) {
    max = -Inf
    for (i in data) {
        if (i > max)
            max = i
    }
    return max
}
```

One way to parallelize this algorithm is to split the data into partitions. If we have a computer with eight CPU cores, we can split the data into eight partitions of 125 million numbers each. Here is the pseudocode for how to perform the same task in parallel:

```
# Run this in parallel across 8 CPU cores
part.results <- run.in.parallel(serialmax(data.part))
# Compute global max
global.max <- serialmax(part.results)
```

This pseudocode runs eight instances of serialmax() in parallel—one for each data partition—to find the local maximum value in each partition. Once all the partitions have been processed, the algorithm finds the global maximum value by finding the largest value among the local maxima. This parallel algorithm works because the global maximum of a dataset must be the largest of the local maxima from all the partitions.

The following figure depicts data parallelism pictorially. The key behind data parallel algorithms is that each partition of data can be processed independently of the other partitions, and the results from all the partitions can be combined to compute the final results. This is similar to the mechanism of the MapReduce framework from Hadoop. Data parallelism allows algorithms to scale up easily as data volume increases—as more data is added to the dataset, more computing nodes can be added to a cluster to process new partitions of data.

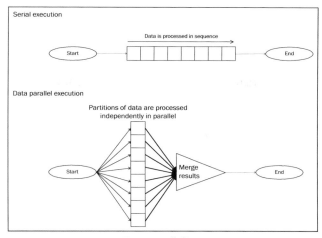

Data parallelism

Other examples of computations and algorithms that can be run in a data parallel way include:

- **Element-wise matrix operations such as addition and subtraction**: The matrices can be partitioned and the operations are applied to each pair of partitions.

- **Means**: The sums and number of elements in each partition can be added to find the global sum and number of elements from which the mean can be computed.

- **K-means clustering**: After data partitioning, the K centroids are distributed to all the partitions. Finding the closest centroid is performed in parallel and independently across the partitions. The centroids are updated by first, calculating the sums and the counts of their respective members in parallel, and then consolidating them in a single process to get the global means.

- **Frequent itemset mining using the Partition algorithm**: In the first pass, the frequent itemsets are mined from each partition of data to generate a global set of candidate itemsets; in the second pass, the supports of the candidate itemsets are summed from each partition to filter out the globally infrequent ones.

The other main class of parallelism is **task parallelism**, where tasks are distributed to and executed on different processors in parallel. The tasks on each processor might be the same or different, and the data that they act on might also be the same or different. The key difference between task parallelism and data parallelism is that the data is not divided into partitions. An example of a task parallel algorithm performing the same task on the same data is the training of a random forest model. A random forest is a collection of decision trees built independently on the same data. During the training process for a particular tree, a random subset of the data is chosen as the training set, and the variables to consider at each branch of the tree are also selected randomly. Hence, even though the same data is used, the trees are different from one another. In order to train a random forest of say 100 decision trees, the workload could be distributed to a computing cluster with 100 processors, with each processor building one tree. All the processors perform the same task on the same data (or exact copies of the data), but the data is not partitioned.

The parallel tasks can also be different. For example, computing a set of summary statistics on the same set of data can be done in a task parallel way. Each process can be assigned to compute a different statistic—the mean, standard deviation, percentiles, and so on.

Pseudocode of a task parallel algorithm might look like this:

```
# Run 4 tasks in parallel across 4 cores
for (task in tasks)
    run.in.parallel(task)
# Collect the results of the 4 tasks
results <- collect.parallel.output()
# Continue processing after all 4 tasks are complete
```

Implementing data parallel algorithms

Several R packages allow code to be executed in parallel. The `parallel` package that comes with R provides the foundation for most parallel computing capabilities in other packages. Let's see how it works with an example.

This example involves finding documents that match a regular expression. Regular expression matching is a fairly computational expensive task, depending on the complexity of the regular expression. The corpus, or set of documents, for this example is a sample of the Reuters-21578 dataset for the topic corporate acquisitions (`acq`) from the `tm` package. Because this dataset contains only 50 documents, they are replicated 100,000 times to form a corpus of 5 million documents so that parallelizing the code will lead to meaningful savings in execution times.

```
library(tm)
```

```
data("acq")
textdata <- rep(sapply(content(acq), content), 1e5)
```

The task is to find documents that match the regular expression \d+(,\d+)? mln dlrs, which represents monetary amounts in millions of dollars. In this regular expression, \d+ matches a string of one or more digits, and (,\d+)? optionally matches a comma followed by one more digits. For example, the strings 12 mln dlrs, 1,234 mln dlrs and 123,456,789 mln dlrs will match the regular expression. First, we will measure the execution time to find these documents serially with grepl():

```
pattern <- "\\d+(,\\d+)? mln dlrs"
system.time(res1 <- grepl(pattern, textdata))
##    user  system elapsed
## 65.601   0.114  65.721
```

Next, we will modify the code to run in parallel and measure the execution time on a computer with four CPU cores:

```
library(parallel)
detectCores()
## [1] 4
cl <- makeCluster(detectCores())
part <- clusterSplit(cl, seq_along(textdata))
text.partitioned <- lapply(part, function(p) textdata[p])
system.time(res2 <- unlist(
    parSapply(cl, text.partitioned, grepl, pattern = pattern)
))
##    user  system elapsed
##  3.708   8.007  50.806
stopCluster(cl)
```

In this code, the detectCores() function reveals how many CPU cores are available on the machine, where this code is executed. Before running any parallel code, makeCluster() is called to create a local cluster of processing nodes with all four CPU cores. The corpus is then split into four partitions using the clusterSplit() function to determine the ideal split of the corpus such that each partition has roughly the same number of documents.

The actual parallel execution of grepl() on each partition of the corpus is carried out by the parSapply() function. Each processing node in the cluster is given a copy of the partition of data that it is supposed to process along with the code to be executed and other variables that are needed to run the code (in this case, the pattern argument). When all four processing nodes have completed their tasks, the results are combined in a similar fashion to sapply().

Finally, the cluster is destroyed by calling stopCluster().

It is good practice to ensure that stopCluster() is always called in production code, even if an error occurs during execution. This can be done as follows:

```
doSomethingInParallel <- function(...) {
    cl <- makeCluster(...)
    on.exit(stopCluster(cl))
    # do something
}
```

In this example, running the task in parallel on four processors resulted in a 23 percent reduction in the execution time. This is not in proportion to the amount of compute resources used to perform the task; with four times as many CPU cores working on it, a perfectly parallelizable task might experience as much as a 75 percent runtime reduction. However, remember Amdahl's law—the speed of parallel code is limited by the serial parts, which includes the overheads of parallelization. In this case, calling makeCluster() with the default arguments creates a **socket-based cluster**. When such a cluster is created, additional copies of R are run as workers. The workers communicate with the master R process using network sockets, hence the name. The worker R processes are initialized with the relevant packages loaded, and data partitions are serialized and sent to each worker process. These overheads can be significant, especially in data parallel algorithms where large volumes of data needs to be transferred to the worker processes.

Besides parSapply(), parallel also provides the parApply() and parLapply() functions; these functions are analogous to the standard sapply(), apply(), and lapply() functions, respectively. In addition, the parLapplyLB() and parSapplyLB() functions provide load balancing, which is useful when the execution of each parallel task takes variable amounts of time. Finally, parRapply() and parCapply() are parallel row and column apply() functions for matrices.

On non-Windows systems, parallel supports another type of cluster that often incurs less overheads—**forked clusters**. In these clusters, new worker processes are forked from the parent R process with a copy of the data. However, the data is not actually copied in the memory unless it is modified by a child process. This means that, compared to socket-based clusters, initializing child processes is quicker and the memory usage is often lower.

Another advantage of using forked clusters is that `parallel` provides a convenient and concise way to run tasks on them via the `mclapply()`, `mcmapply()`, and `mcMap()` functions. (These functions start with `mc` because they were originally a part of the `multicore` package) There is no need to explicitly create and destroy the cluster, as these functions do this automatically. We can simply call `mclapply()` and state the number of worker processes to fork via the `mc.cores` argument:

```
system.time(res3 <- unlist(
    mclapply(text.partitioned, grepl, pattern = pattern,
             mc.cores = detectCores())
))
##     user  system elapsed
## 127.012   0.350  33.264
```

This shows a 49 percent reduction in execution time compared to the serial version, and 35 percent reduction compared to parallelizing using a socket-based cluster. For this example, forked clusters provide the best performance.

 Due to differences in system configuration, you might see very different results when you try the examples in this chapter in your own environment. When you develop parallel code, it is important to test the code in an environment that is similar to the one that it will eventually run in.

Implementing task parallel algorithms

Let's now see how to implement a task parallel algorithm using both socket-based and forked clusters. We will look at how to run the same task and different tasks on workers in a cluster.

Running the same task on workers in a cluster

To demonstrate how to run the same task on a cluster, the task for this example is to generate 500 million Poisson random numbers. We will do this by using L'Ecuyer's combined multiple-recursive generator, which is the only random number generator in base R that supports multiple streams to generate random numbers in parallel. The random number generator is selected by calling the `RNGkind()` function.

We cannot just use any random number generator in parallel because the randomness of the data depends on the algorithm used to generate random data and the seed value given to each parallel task. Most other algorithms were not designed to produce random numbers in multiple parallel streams, and might produce multiple highly correlated streams of numbers, or worse, multiple identical streams!

First, we will measure the execution time of the serial algorithm:

```
RNGkind("L'Ecuyer-CMRG")
nsamples <- 5e8
lambda <- 10
system.time(random1 <- rpois(nsamples, lambda))
##    user  system elapsed
## 51.905   0.636  52.544
```

To generate the random numbers on a cluster, we will first distribute the task evenly among the workers. In the following code, the integer vector samples.per.process contains the number of random numbers that each worker needs to generate on a four-core CPU. The seq() function produces ncores+1 numbers evenly distributed between 0 and nsamples, with the first number being 0 and the next ncores numbers indicating the approximate cumulative number of samples across the worker processes. The round() function rounds off these numbers into integers and diff() computes the difference between them to give the number of random numbers that each worker process should generate.

```
cores <- detectCores()
cl <- makeCluster(ncores)
samples.per.process <-
    diff(round(seq(0, nsamples, length.out = ncores+1)))
```

Before we can generate the random numbers on a cluster, each worker needs a different seed from which it can generate a stream of random numbers. The seeds need to be set on all the workers before running the task, to ensure that all the workers generate different random numbers.

For a socket-based cluster, we can call clusterSetRNGStream() to set the seeds for the workers, then run the random number generation task on the cluster. When the task is completed, we call stopCluster() to shut down the cluster:

```
clusterSetRNGStream(cl)
system.time(random2 <- unlist(
```

```
    parLapply(cl, samples.per.process, rpois,
              lambda = lambda)
))
##  user  system elapsed
## 5.006   3.000  27.436
stopCluster(cl)
```

Using four parallel processes in a socket-based cluster reduces the execution time by 48 percent. The performance of this type of cluster for this example is better than that of the data parallel example because there is less data to copy to the worker processes—only an integer that indicates how many random numbers to generate.

Next, we run the same task on a forked cluster (again, this is not supported on Windows). The mclapply() function can set the random number seeds for each worker for us, when the mc.set.seed argument is set to TRUE; we do not need to call clusterSetRNGStream(). Otherwise, the code is similar to that of the socket-based cluster:

```
system.time(random3 <- unlist(
    mclapply(samples.per.process, rpois,
             lambda = lambda,
             mc.set.seed = TRUE, mc.cores = ncores)
))
##   user  system elapsed
## 76.283   7.272  25.052
```

On our test machine, the execution time of the forked cluster is slightly faster, but close to that of the socket-based cluster, indicating that the overheads for this task are similar for both types of clusters.

Running different tasks on workers in a cluster

So far, we have executed the same tasks on each parallel process. The *parallel* package also allows different tasks to be executed on different workers. For this example, the task is to generate not only Poisson random numbers, but also uniform, normal, and exponential random numbers. As before, we start by measuring the time to perform this task serially:

```
RNGkind("L'Ecuyer-CMRG")
nsamples <- 5e7
pois.lambda <- 10
system.time(random1 <- list(pois = rpois(nsamples,
```

```
                                        pois.lambda),
                        unif = runif(nsamples),
                        norm = rnorm(nsamples),
                        exp = rexp(nsamples)))
##   user  system elapsed
## 14.180   0.384  14.570
```

In order to run different tasks on different workers on socket-based clusters, a list of function calls and their associated arguments must be passed to parLapply(). This is a bit cumbersome, but parallel unfortunately does not provide an easier interface to run different tasks on a socket-based cluster. In the following code, the function calls are represented as a list of lists, where the first element of each sublist is the name of the function that runs on a worker, and the second element contains the function arguments. The function do.call() is used to call the given function with the given arguments.

```
cores <- detectCores()
cl <- makeCluster(cores)
calls <- list(pois = list("rpois", list(n = nsamples,
                                        lambda = pois.lambda)),
              unif = list("runif", list(n = nsamples)),
              norm = list("rnorm", list(n = nsamples)),
              exp = list("rexp", list(n = nsamples)))
clusterSetRNGStream(cl)
system.time(
    random2 <- parLapply(cl, calls,
                         function(call) {
                             do.call(call[[1]], call[[2]])
                         })
)
##   user  system elapsed
## 2.185   1.629  10.403
stopCluster(cl)
```

On forked clusters on non-Windows machines, the mcparallel() and mccollect() functions offer a more intuitive way to run different tasks on different workers. For each task, mcparallel() sends the given task to an available worker. Once all the workers have been assigned their tasks, mccollect() waits for the workers to complete their tasks and collects the results from all the workers.

```
mc.reset.stream()
system.time({
    jobs <- list()
    jobs[[1]] <- mcparallel(rpois(nsamples, pois.lambda),
```

```
                                    "pois", mc.set.seed = TRUE)
      jobs[[2]] <- mcparallel(runif(nsamples),
                                    "unif", mc.set.seed = TRUE)
      jobs[[3]] <- mcparallel(rnorm(nsamples),
                                    "norm", mc.set.seed = TRUE)
      jobs[[4]] <- mcparallel(rexp(nsamples),
                                    "exp", mc.set.seed = TRUE)
      random3 <- mccollect(jobs)
   })
   ##    user  system elapsed
   ## 14.535   3.569   7.972
```

Notice that we also had to call mc.reset.stream() to set the seeds for random number generation in each worker. This was not necessary when we used mclapply(), which calls mc.reset.stream() for us. However, mcparallel() does not, so we need to call it ourselves.

Executing tasks in parallel on a cluster of computers

By using the parallel package, we are not limited to running parallel code on a single computer; we can also do it on a cluster of computers. This allows much larger computational tasks to be performed, irrespective of whether we use data parallelism or task parallelism. Only socket-based clusters can be used for this purpose, as processes cannot be forked onto a different computer.

There are many ways to set up a cluster of computers to work with R. To keep things simple, all computers in the cluster should have the same configuration for R—the same version of R, installed in the same directories, installed with the same versions of any packages required, and running on the same operating system. The examples in this section have been tested on a cluster of three computers running Ubuntu 14.04—one master node and two worker nodes.

The master and worker nodes should be on the same network and able to communicate with each other via SSH (port 22) and one other port for exchanging data and code. This communications port can be set with the R_PARALLEL_PORT environment variable. If it is not set, R will randomly choose a port in the range 11000 to 11999.

By default, SSH is used to launch R on the workers. First, ensure that the SSH server is set up and running on all the worker nodes.

For Windows worker nodes, download and install Cygwin from `http://www.cygwin.com`. When prompted to install additional packages, install the `openssh` package. Then, right-click on the **Cygwin** icon and select **Run as Administrator**. In the terminal window that opens, run the following code to set up the SSH server. The `ssh-host-config` command configures the SSH server with the default settings. The `chmod 400` command sets the permissions on the generated security keys so that only the user who owns the keys can read them, and `cygrunsrv -S sshd` starts the SSH server.

```
$ ssh-host-config -y -c "tty ntsec"
$ chmod 400 /etc/ssh_*_key
$ cygrunsrv -S sshd
```

Other operating systems like Linux normally come with an installed SSH server. Consult the documentation of your operating system for how to set it up.

The master node should be able to connect to the worker nodes using key-based authentication, as using password-based authentication to run a cluster might not always work. Use the following commands to set up key-based authentication. Windows users should run this from within a Cygwin terminal.

```
# Run all these commands on the master node
# Generate an RSA key pair without password
$ ssh-keygen -t rsa
$ chmod 400 .ssh/id_rsa
# Copy public key to worker node (run for every worker)
$ ssh-copy-id -i .ssh/id_rsa.pub worker_username@worker_address
# Test connection (run for every worker)
$ ssh worker_username@worker_address
# You should be able to log in without entering a password
```

Once all the computers are set up, we can run parallel tasks on the cluster just as before. The only change needed is in the call to `makeCluster()`, where the IP addresses or domain names of the worker nodes must be provided instead of the number of workers to create local workers. In the following example, replace the IP addresses with the IP addresses of your master and worker nodes.

```
workers <- c("192.168.213.225", "192.168.213.226")
nworkers <- length(workers)
cl <- makeCluster(workers, master = "192.168.213.138")
```

If you are having trouble to start the cluster by automatically using `makeCluster()`, add the `manual=TRUE` argument to the call to `makeCluster()`, then follow the instructions given, to start the worker processes on each of the worker nodes.

The code that sends the tasks to the workers for execution is then the same as before:

```
clusterSetRNGStream(cl)
samples.per.process <- c(2.5e8, 2.5e8)
lambda <- 10
random <- unlist(
    parLapply(cl, samples.per.process,
              function(n, lambda) rpois(n, lambda),
              lambda)
)
stopCluster(cl)
```

Because a cluster of computers has to communicate over a network, the bandwidth and latency of the network connections play a critical role in the performance of the whole cluster. It is best that the nodes are in the same location, connected by a high-speed network where data and code can be exchanged between the master and worker nodes speedily.

Shared memory versus distributed memory parallelism

In the examples that we have seen so far, data is copied from the master process or node to each worker. This is called **distributed memory** parallelism, where each process has its own memory space. In other words, each process needs to have its own copy of the data that it needs to work on, even if multiple processes are working on the same data. This is the typical way to distribute data in a cluster of computers because the workers in the cluster cannot access each other's RAM, so they need their own copy of the data.

However, this can result in huge redundancies when you run a parallel code on multiple processes on a single computer. If a dataset takes up 5 GB of memory, then running four parallel processes could result in five copies of the data in memory—one for the master and four for the workers—occupying a total of 25 GB. Earlier, we saw that forked clusters might not suffer from this problem, as most operating systems do not make copies of the data in the memory unless it is modified by one of the workers. However, this is not guaranteed. On socket-based clusters, because new instances of R are created, new copies of the data are made for each worker.

Contrast this with **shared memory** parallelism, where all the workers share a single copy of the data. This not only saves the memory, but also reduces the time needed to initialize and shut down the cluster, as the data does not need to be copied.

Although the `parallel` package does not provide support for shared memory parallelism by default, we can achieve it by using the right data structures. One example for this is `big.matrix` from the `bigmemory` package that we learned about in the previous chapter (not available for Windows at the time of writing). In *Chapter 7, Processing Large Datasets with Limited RAM*, we used `big.matrix` for its memory-mapped file capabilities; in this chapter, we will take advantage of it as a shared memory object for parallel workers. Besides taking the form of memory-mapped files on disk, `big.matrix` objects can also be fully in-memory objects that behave just like standard R matrices. The key difference is that `big.matrix` objects are not copied according to the usual R rules for copying objects that we examined in *Chapter 6, Simple Tweaks to Use Less RAM*. Instead, they are only copied when a call to `deepcopy()` is made. Let's see what this looks like in practice. First, we will create a `big.matrix` a, then a new variable b that points to a.

```
library(bigmemory)
a <- big.matrix(3, 3)
a[, ]
##       [,1] [,2] [,3]
## [1,]   NA   NA   NA
## [2,]   NA   NA   NA
## [3,]   NA   NA   NA
b <- a
b[, ]
##       [,1] [,2] [,3]
## [1,]   NA   NA   NA
## [2,]   NA   NA   NA
## [3,]   NA   NA   NA
```

Next, we will modify the contents of b. Under R's normal data copying rules, the data should be copied in the memory so that the contents of a are not modified. However, that is not the case:

```
b[, ] <- diag(3)
b[, ]
##       [,1] [,2] [,3]
## [1,]    1    0    0
## [2,]    0    1    0
## [3,]    0    0    1
```

```
a[, ]
##      [,1] [,2] [,3]
## [1,]    1    0    0
## [2,]    0    1    0
## [3,]    0    0    1
```

Clearly, a and b are the same object. A peek under their hoods at their pointers to the data confirms this:

```
a
## An object of class "big.matrix"
## Slot "address":
## <pointer: 0x7fab5e2b8750>
b
## An object of class "big.matrix"
## Slot "address":
## <pointer: 0x7fab5e2b8750>
```

Now, let's see how this impacts the performance of parallel code. This example uses a matrix with two variables and 50 million observations and the equivalent big.matrix:

```
r <- 5e7
m <- matrix(rnorm(r * 2), r, 2)
bm <- as.big.matrix(m)
```

The task here is to compute the absolute difference for each pair of numbers. First, we will measure the execution time using a socket-based cluster on the matrix:

```
cl <- makeCluster(detectCores())
part <- clusterSplit(cl, seq_len(r))
system.time(res <- unlist(
    parLapply(cl, part,
              function(part, data) {
                  abs(data[part, 1] - data[part, 2])
              },
              m)
))
## user    system elapsed
## 5.199   1.856  10.590
stopCluster(cl)
```

It took 10.6 seconds on four CPU cores, and each thread consumed 1.01 GB of RAM, as shown in the following screenshot taken from Mac OS X's Activity Monitor:

Process Name		Memory	Real Mem ▼	Private Mem	Shared Mem
	rsession	2.47 GB	3.90 GB	3.22 GB	10.8 MB
	R	1.01 GB	1.01 GB	1.00 GB	10.8 MB
	R	1.00 GB	1.01 GB	1.00 GB	10.8 MB
	R	1.01 GB	1.01 GB	1.01 GB	10.8 MB
	R	1.01 GB	1.01 GB	1.01 GB	10.8 MB

Memory consumption of socket-based cluster using matrix data

Now, let's use `big.matrix` to see if there is a difference in speed and memory efficiency. In order to pass `big.matrix` to each worker process, we need to use `describe()` to pass the metadata of `big.matrix` to each process. Within each process, `attach.big.matrix()` must be called to access `big.matrix`. Also notice that `library(bigmemory)` is called within the function. This is required because each worker is a new R process so any packages required to run the task must be loaded on the workers as well.

```
cl <- makeCluster(detectCores())
system.time(res2 <- unlist(
    parLapply(cl, part,
            function(part, data.desc) {
                library(bigmemory)
                data <- attach.big.matrix(data.desc)
                abs(data[part, 1] - data[part, 2])
            },
            describe(bm))
))
##   user   system elapsed
## 1.278   0.692   2.956
stopCluster(cl)
```

This version ran must faster with a 72 percent saving in the execution time from not making copies of the matrix! Furthermore, each R process took up only about 373 MB of memory, as shown in the following figure in the `Private Mem` column. 774 MB of the memory was shared from the parent process, most of which was the `big.matrix` object.

Process Name		Memory	Real Mem ▼	Private Mem	Shared Mem
	rsession	2.47 GB	3.90 GB	2.47 GB	774.0 MB
	R	373.8 MB	571.2 MB	373.0 MB	774.0 MB
	R	374.1 MB	570.2 MB	373.2 MB	774.0 MB
	R	371.8 MB	569.3 MB	371.0 MB	774.0 MB
	R	373.0 MB	569.2 MB	372.2 MB	774.0 MB

Memory consumption of forked cluster using big.matrix data.

Shared memory parallelism worked in this case because the worker processed only read from the data but did not write to it. Designing parallel algorithms that write to shared memory is much trickier and outside the scope of this book. Much care must be take to avoid **race conditions**, which are conflicts and programming errors that arise when worker processes that read from and write to the same memory locations are not properly coordinated. This can lead to the data being corrupted.

Optimizing parallel performance

Throughout the examples in this chapter, we saw various factors that affect the performance of parallel code.

One overhead in running a parallel R code is in setting up the cluster. By default, `makeCluster()` instructs the worker processes to load the `methods` package when they start. This can take a good amount of time, so if the task to be run does not require *methods*, this behavior can be disabled by passing `methods=FALSE` to `makeCluster()`.

One of the biggest obstacles to parallel performance is the copying and transmission of data between the master process and the worker process. This obstacle can be large when you run parallel tasks on a cluster of computers, as many factors such as limited network bandwidth, and data encryption slow down the transmission of data even before any computations can be done. Even on a single computer, unnecessary copying of data in memory takes up precious seconds that can multiply as the data grows. This can also happen the other way around, for example in the random number generation examples, where the input data is small but the output is large.

One way to minimize these data communication overheads is to use shared memory objects, as we saw in the preceding section. Data compression can also help in some circumstances, provided the computational time to compress and decompress the data is relatively short. Another option is to store the data, including the results of any intermediate computations, at each worker node, and reserve internode data communication to only what is required to coordinate the tasks. An example of this is MapReduce from Hadoop, which we will explore in *Chapter 10, R and Big Data*.

Although there are ways to minimize the costs of data communication, sometimes these overheads far exceed the gains from parallelization, and we are better off running the code in series. It can be difficult to calculate the trade-offs between the performance gains and increased overheads of parallelizing code. When in doubt, conduct small experiments like we have done in this chapter.

Summary

In this chapter, we learned about two classes of parallelism: data parallelism and task parallelism. Data parallelism is good for tasks that can be performed in parallel on partitions of a dataset. The dataset to be processed is split into partitions and each partition is processed on a different worker processes. Task parallelism, on the other hand, divides a set of similar or different tasks to amongst the worker processes. In either case, Amdahl's law states that the maximum improvement in speed that can be achieved by parallelizing code is limited by the proportion of that code that can be parallelized.

R supports both types of parallelism using the *parallel* package. We learned how to implement both data parallel and task parallel algorithms using socket-based clusters and forked clusters. We also learned how to run tasks in parallel on a cluster of computers using socket-based clusters.

The examples in this chapter demonstrated that the improvement in performance by parallelizing code depends on a great variety of factors—the type of cluster, whether the task is run on a single computer or on a cluster, the volume of data exchanged between nodes, the complexity of the individual subtasks, and so on. While techniques such as shared-memory parallelism can mitigate some of the bottlenecks, parallel computing is a complex discipline that takes much experience and skill to get well executed. Used correctly, the payoffs in speed and efficiency can be significant.

For a deeper look at parallel computing in R, see *Parallel R* by Q. Ethan McCallum and Stephen Weston.

In the next chapter, we will look beyond the boundaries of R to tap on the processing power of specialized data processing platforms like analytical databases.

9

Offloading Data Processing to Database Systems

We have learned many different ways to optimize the performance of an R code for speed and memory efficiency. But sometimes R alone is not enough. Perhaps, a very large dataset is stored in a data warehouse. It would be infeasible to extract all the data into R for processing. We might even wish to tap into the power of specially-designed analytical databases that can perform computations on data much more efficiently than R can. In this chapter, we will learn how to tap into the power of external database systems from within R and combine that power with the flexibility and ease of use of the R language.

This chapter covers the following:

- Extracting data into R versus processing data in a database
- Preprocessing data in a relational database using SQL
- Converting R expressions into SQL
- Running statistical and machine learning algorithms in a database
- Using columnar databases for improved performance
- Using array databases for maximum scientific computing performance

Extracting data into R versus processing data in a database

Most R programmers are familiar with and very comfortable manipulating data in R using R data structures and packages. This requires moving all the data into R whether in memory or on a disk, on a single computer or on a cluster. In some situations, this might not be efficient especially if the data constantly changes and needs to be updated often—extracting data out of a database or data warehouse every time it needs to be analyzed takes a lot of time and computational resources. In some cases, it might not be feasible at all to move terabytes or more of data from their sources into R.

Instead of moving the data into R, another approach is to move the computational tasks to the data. In other words, we can process the data in the database and retrieve only the results into R, which are usually much smaller than the raw data. This reduces the amount of network bandwidth required to transmit the data and the local storage and memory required to process the data in R. It also allows R programmers to tap into powerful databases that are purpose-built for analytical workloads on large datasets.

In order to perform in-database computations and analyses, a new set of tools is needed. At the foundation of all in-database tools is the SQL language, which most relational databases support. While this book is not about SQL, knowing how to run even simple SQL statements in a database can help speed up many tasks in R. Other tools such as `dplyr` build on SQL to provide easy and familiar interfaces such as data frame-like objects in order to manipulate the data in the database. Yet other tools like MonetDB.R and SciDB allow us to tap into databases that are designed for high-performance analytical workloads such as columnar and array databases. We shall look at these tools in the following sections.

Preprocessing data in a relational database using SQL

We will start by learning how to run SQL statements in the database from R. The first few examples show how processing data in a database instead of moving all the data into R can result in faster performance even for simple operations.

To run the examples in this chapter, you will need a database server supported by R. The CRAN package, `RJDBC` provides an interface to JDBC drivers that most databases come with. Alternatively, search on CRAN for packages such as `RPostgreSQL`, `RMySQL`, and `ROracle` that offer functionalities and optimizations specific to each database.

The following examples are based on a PostgreSQL database and the RPostgreSQL package as we will need them later in this chapter when we learn about the PivotalR package and MADlib software. Feel free, however, to adapt the code to the database that you use.

Configuring PostgreSQL to work with R involves setting up both the server and the client. First, we need to set up the PostgreSQL database server. This can be on a different computer than the one running R to simulate tapping into an existing database from R; or it can be on the same computer for simplicity. In our case, we will set up a Linux virtual machine to host the PostgreSQL database server and use Mac OS X as the client. Here are the steps to set up the database server:

1. Download PostgreSQL from `http://www.postgresql.org/download/` and follow the installation instructions for your operating system.

2. Enable username/password authentication on the database server by adding the following command line to `pg_hba.conf` (in the PostgreSQL data folder):

    ```
    host    all    all    0.0.0.0/0    md5
    ```

3. Create a user account and password that can be used to connect to the database from R by running the following command line (you might need to be the `root` or the `postgres` user to run this):

    ```
    $ createuser  --pwprompt ruser
    ```

4. Create a database for the examples in this chapter by running the following command line (you might need to be the `root` or the `postgres` user to run this):

    ```
    $ createdb --owner=ruser rdb
    ```

5. Ensure that the database is accessible via a network connection from the computer that runs R by adding the following lines to `postgresql.conf` (in the PostgreSQL data folder):

    ```
    listen_address = '*'
    port = 5432
    ```

6. Restart the PostgreSQL server for the changes to take effect (you might need to be the `root` user to do this).

Next, we will set up the client by installing the RPostgreSQL package on the computer that runs R:

1. Non-Windows only: install libpq, the PostgreSQL C libraries, that are needed to install RPostgreSQL. If you have installed the PostgreSQL server on the same computer as R, the libraries are already in the system, so you can skip this step. Otherwise, make sure that the version of the libraries matches the version of the PostgreSQL server:

```
# On Mac OS X (using Homebrew)
$ brew install postgresql
# On Debian / Ubuntu
$ sudo apt-get install libpq-dev
# On Redhat / CentOS
$ sudo yum install postgresql-devel
# On Windows: this step is not needed
```

2. Run R and install the RPostgreSQL CRAN package from its source code:

```
# On platforms other than Windows
install.packages("RPostgreSQL", type="source")
# On Windows
install.packages("RPostgreSQL")
```

3. Test the database connection from R by substituting the details with the correct information for your database:

```
library(RPostgreSQL)
db.drv <- PostgreSQL()
db.conn <- dbConnect(db.drv, host = "hostname",
                     port = 5432, dbname = "rdb",
                     user = "ruser",
                     password = "rpassword")
dbListTables(db.conn)
## character(0)
```

Once the database is set up, we will generate some sales data for the examples to follow. The example database has two tables, sales and trans_items. The sales table contains information about sales transactions in a retail chain, including the transaction ID, customer ID, and store ID. The trans_items table records the individual items in each transaction and the total price for each item. Once the data is generated in R, we will use dbWriteTable() to write the data into new tables in the database, as follows:

```
ntrans <- 1e5
ncust <- 1e4
```

```
nstore <- 100
sales <- data.frame(
    trans_id = seq_len(ntrans),
    cust_id = sample.int(ncust, ntrans, TRUE),
    store_id = sample.int(nstore, ntrans, TRUE))
dbWriteTable(db.conn, "sales", sales)
trans.lengths <- rpois(ntrans, 3) + 1L
trans.items <- data.frame(
    trans_id = rep.int(seq_len(ntrans), trans.lengths),
    item_id = unlist(lapply(trans.lengths, sample.int, n = 1000)),
    price = exp(rnorm(sum(trans.lengths))))
dbWriteTable(db.conn, "trans_items", trans.items)
```

The first task is to calculate the total sales for each store. Let's compare two different ways of doing this. The first way is to extract all the store IDs along with the prices of the items associated with each store by joining the sales and trans_items tables. Once this data is in R, the sales for each store is computed by summing the item prices for each store ID using tapply(). The second way to compute the same data is to perform the aggregation in the database using the SQL GROUP BY clause and SUM() function. We will use microbenchmark() to compare the execution times for both methods:

```
library(microbenchmark)
microbenchmark({
    res <- dbGetQuery(
        db.conn,
        'SELECT store_id, price
        FROM sales INNER JOIN trans_items USING (trans_id);')
    res <- tapply(res$price, res$store_id, sum)
}, times = 10)
## Unit: milliseconds
##       min       lq   median       uq      max neval
##  740.7533 745.2563 771.3706 775.3665 780.3819    10
microbenchmark({
    res <- dbGetQuery(
        db.conn,
        'SELECT store_id, SUM(price) as total_sales
        FROM sales INNER JOIN trans_items USING (trans_id)
        GROUP BY store_id;')
}, times = 10)
## Unit: milliseconds
##      min       lq   median       uq      max neval
##  244.779 248.6401 251.1465 255.3652 279.6666    10
```

In this simple test, performing the computations in the database takes only 33 percent of the time to do the same by extracting the data into R. Let's take a look at another example. The second task is to get a list of the top ten customers who have spent the most money, in decreasing order. Again, we will compare the speed of performing the computations in R versus in the database:

```
microbenchmark({
    res <- dbGetQuery(
        db.conn,
        'SELECT cust_id, price
        FROM sales INNER JOIN trans_items USING (trans_id);')
    res <- tapply(res$price, res$cust_id, sum)
    res <- sort(res, decreasing = TRUE)
    res <- head(res, 10L)
}, times = 10)
## Unit: milliseconds
##       min       lq    median       uq      max neval
##  814.2492 828.7774  843.1869 846.4235 952.1318    10
microbenchmark({
    res <- dbGetQuery(
        db.conn,
        'SELECT cust_id, SUM(price) as spending
        FROM sales INNER JOIN trans_items USING (trans_id)
        GROUP BY cust_id
        ORDER BY spending DESC
        LIMIT 10;')
}, times = 10)
## Unit: milliseconds
##       min       lq    median       uq      max neval
##  259.1621 260.5494  260.9566 265.1368 294.1732    10
```

Again, running the computations in the database instead of in R has resulted in a 70 percent reduction in the execution time.

Once we are done, we need to disconnect from the database:

```
dbDisconnect(db.conn)
```

These tests were conducted on the same computer with the database server running in a virtual machine. Even on such a small dataset and over a very small network (the virtual network between the host computer and the virtual machine), the differences in the performance were dramatic. These tests clearly demonstrate that minimizing the amount of data being copied out of the database can provide a big performance boost. On larger datasets and powerful analytical databases, the performance difference can be even more pronounced.

Converting R expressions to SQL

While SQL is a powerful and flexible language used to manipulate data in a databa not everyone is proficient in it. Fortunately, the R community has developed a few packages that translate familiar R syntax into SQL statements that are then executed on the database. We will look at two of them—dplyr and PivotalR.

Using dplyr

The dplyr package is a handy package designed to allow the manipulation of table-like data with a standard set of operations and transformations, no matter where the data is stored—in a data frame, data table, or database. It supports SQLite, PostgreSQL, MySQL, Amazon RedShift, Google BigQuery, and MonetDB databases.

The dplyr package provides a way to specify a set of operations to be performed on the data without actually performing the computations on the database server until we instruct R to do so, by calling the collect() function. By pooling a few operations together (as opposed to executing them one by one), the database server can optimize the execution. This in turn helps to minimize computational load of the server. Let's see how this works with an example.

First, we need to establish a connection with the database, as before. Here, we will use the src_postgres() function provided by dplyr. The syntax is slightly different from dbConnect() of RPostgreSQL, but the arguments are similar. After establishing the connection, we will create references to the sales and trans_items tables in the database using the tbl() function:

```
library(dplyr)
db.conn <- src_postgres(dbname = "rdb", host = "hostname",
                        port = 5432, user = "ruser",
                        password = "rpassword")
sales.tb <- tbl(db.conn, "sales")
trans_items.tb <- tbl(db.conn, "trans_items")
```

Let's recreate the previous example using dplyr:

```
joined.tb <- inner_join(sales.tb, trans_items.tb, by = "trans_id")
cust.items <- group_by(joined.tb, cust_id)
cust.spending <- summarize(cust.items, spending = sum(price))
cust.spending <- arrange(cust.spending, desc(spending))
cust.spending <- select(cust.spending, cust_id, spending)
```

The first step is to join the `sales` and `trans_items` tables using `inner_join()`. Then, `group_by()` groups the items according to customer ID, and `summarize()` sums the total spending for each customer. Finally, we will use `arrange()` to sort the customer in decreasing order of spending, and `select()` to select only the columns we want.

The output of each of these steps is a `tbl` object:

```
class(cust.spending)
## [1] "tbl_postgres" "tbl_sql"      "tbl"
```

These are virtual tables that are an accumulation of all the operations applied so far. Up to this point, no SQL has been sent to the database server and no computation has been performed on it. We can examine the SQL query that will be executed when the results are retrieved by retrieving the `query` member of the `tbl` object:

```
cust.spending$query
## <Query> SELECT "cust_id" AS "cust_id", "spending" AS "spending"
## FROM (SELECT "cust_id", SUM("price") AS "spending"
## FROM (SELECT "row.names" AS "row.names.x", "trans_id" AS
## "trans_id", "cust_id" AS "cust_id", "store_id" AS "store_id"
## FROM "sales") AS "nsthygziij"
##
## INNER JOIN
##
## (SELECT "row.names" AS "row.names.y", "trans_id" AS "trans_id",
## "item_id" AS "item_id", "price" AS "price"
## FROM "trans_items") AS "cuwpqadrgf"
##
## USING ("trans_id")
## GROUP BY "cust_id") AS "_W8"
## ORDER BY "spending" DESC
## <PostgreSQLConnection:(11726,2)>
```

Normally, the `collect()` function is used to run the SQL statement and retrieve the results:

```
custs.by.spending <- collect(cust.spending)
```

Since we want only the top 10 customers and not all the customers, we can use `head()` to minimize the data being transferred from the database into R:

```
top.custs <- head(cust.spending, 10L)
```

As more complex data manipulation operations are constructed in dplyr, the individual R statements and temporary variables created can get unwieldy. The dplyr package provides the %>% operator to chain operations together. The preceding construct can be rewritten more succinctly as:

```
top.custs <-
    sales.tb %>% inner_join(trans_items.tb, by = "trans_id") %>%
    group_by(cust_id) %>%
    summarize(spending = sum(price)) %>%
    arrange(desc(spending)) %>%
    select(cust_id, spending) %>%
    head(10L)
```

The dplyr package provides other useful operations like filter() for filtering rows, and mutate() for defining new columns as functions of the existing columns. These operations can be combined in many creative and useful ways to process data in a database before retrieving the results into R.

Using PivotalR

The PivotalR package provides similar capabilities as dplyr, but with a different syntax. Because it was developed by Pivotal Software Inc., it supports only PostgreSQL or Pivotal (Greenplum) databases.

As usual, the first step in using the package is to establish a connection to the database:

```
library(PivotalR)
db.conn <- db.connect(host = "hostname", port = 5432,
                      dbname = "rdb", user = "ruser",
                      password = "rpassword")
```

> If you have not installed MADlib on the PostgreSQL database (see the next section of this chapter), you might get a warning that says "MADlib does not exist in database." This is not a problem for the examples in this section as they do not cover the MADlib functions.

The next step is to create references to the database tables using db.data.frame():

```
sales.tb <- db.data.frame("sales", db.conn)
trans_items.tb <- db.data.frame("trans_items", db.conn)
```

The db.data.frame objects behave similar to standard R data frames in many ways, except that they are wrappers for SQL queries that need to be executed on the database. Many of the standard R information and statistical functions are supported. In order to execute the SQL and retrieve the results, use the lookat() function (or the shorthand lk()). For example:

```
dim(sales.tb)
## [1] 1e+05 4e+00
names(sales.tb)
## [1] "row.names" "trans_id"  "cust_id"   "store_id"
lookat(count(sales.tb$cust_id))
## [1] 1e+05
lookat(min(trans_items.tb$price))
## [1] 0.009554177
lookat(max(trans_items.tb$price))
## [1] 121.3909
```

To see the SQL query that will be executed on the database server, use the content() method:

```
content(max(trans_items.tb$price))
## [1] "select max(\"price\") as \"price_max\"
## from \"trans_items\""
```

> If you get the error message "Invalid SciDB object", it could mean that some of the PivotalR functions are being masked by functions of the same name in the SciDB package, which we will cover later in this chapter. In particular, both packages provide the count() function. To run the examples in this section successfully, unload the scidb package with detach("package:scidb", unload=TRUE).

New columns can be computed from existing columns by using the familiar R syntax without affecting the data on the database; instead, the transformations are translated into SQL functions that compute the new columns on the fly. In the following example, we will compute a new column foreign_price that is returned to R in memory and not stored in the database:

```
trans_items.tb$foreign_price <- trans_items.tb$price * 1.25
content(trans_items.tb)
```

```
## [1] "select \"row.names\" as \"row.names\", \"trans_id\" as
## \"trans_id\", \"item_id\" as \"item_id\", \"price\" as
## \"price\", (\"price\") * (1.25) as \"foreign_price\" from
## \"trans_items\""
```

Let's take a look at a full example of how to construct a query in PivotalR. Say we want to compute some statistics to understand the purchasing patterns of consumers at the transaction level. We have to group the data by transactions and then group it again by customers to compute the statistics for each customer:

```
trans <- by(trans_items.tb["price"], trans_items.tb$trans_id, sum)
sales.value <- merge(sales.tb[c("trans_id", "cust_id",
                                "store_id")],
                 trans, by = "trans_id")
cust.sales <- by(sales.value, sales.value$cust_id,
                 function(x) {
                     trans_count <- count(x$trans_id)
                     total_spend <- sum(x$price_sum)
                     stores_visited <- count(x$store_id)
                     cbind(trans_count, total_spend,
                         stores_visited)
                 })
names(cust.sales) <- c("cust_id", "trans_count", "total_spend",
                     "stores_visited")
lookat(cust.sales, 5)
##   cust_id trans_count total_spend stores_visited
## 1       1           9    44.73121              9
## 2       2           7    41.90196              7
## 3       3          13    87.37564             13
## 4       4          11    58.34653             11
## 5       5          15    95.09015             15
```

The first call to by() aggregates the item-level sales data into transactions; summing up the total value of each transaction. Next, merge() joins the sales table with the aggregated transaction data to match the customers with how much they have spent. Then, we will use by() again to aggregate all the transactions by customer. For each customer, we will calculate the number of transactions they made, the total value of those transactions, and the number of stores they visited.

Instead of returning the results, they can also be stored into a new database table by using `as.db.data.frame()`. This is useful for lengthy computations with many intermediate steps. Storing intermediate results in the database helps to reduce the amount of data being transferred between R and the database.

```
cust_sales.tb <- as.db.data.frame(cust.sales, "cust_sales")
```

Further statistics can be computed from the intermediate data, such as the minimum, maximum, mean and standard deviation of customer spending:

```
lookat(min(cust_sales.tb$total_spend))
## [1]  0.4961619
lookat(max(cust_sales.tb$total_spend))
## [1]  227.8077
lookat(mean(cust_sales.tb$total_spend))
## [1]  66.16597
lookat(sd(cust_sales.tb$total_spend))
## [1]  26.71887
```

When the intermediate data is no longer required, it can be deleted from the database:

```
delete(cust_sales.tb)
```

Both `dplyr` and `PivotalR` provide flexible easy ways to manipulate data in a database using R functions and syntax. They allow us to tap into the processing power and speed of high-performance databases to query large datasets and integrate the results of the queries into other analyses in R. Because they are quite similar in capabilities, choosing between the two is largely a matter of compatibility with existing database systems and personal preference for one syntax over the other.

Running statistical and machine learning algorithms in a database

So far, the examples in this chapter have performed simple computations on data in a database. Sometimes we need to perform more complex computations than that. Several database vendors have begun to build advanced statistics or even machine learning capabilities into their database products, allowing these advanced algorithms to run in the database using highly optimized code for maximum performance. In this chapter, we will look at one open source project, MADlib (http://madlib.net/), whose development is supported by Pivotal Inc., that brings advanced statistics and machine learning capabilities to PostgreSQL databases.

MADlib adds a host of statistical capabilities to PostgreSQL, including descriptive statistics, hypothesis tests, array arithmetic, probability functions, dimensionality reduction, linear models, clustering models, association rules, and text analysis. New models and statistical methods are constantly being added to the library to expand its capabilities.

 At the moment, MADlib binaries are only available for Mac OS X and Red Hat/CentOS Linux. For other operating systems, https:// github.com/madlib/madlib/wiki/Building-MADlib-from-Source provides instructions to build MADlib from source. MADlib does not support Windows at the time of writing.

Before installing MADlib, ensure that the `plpython` module from PostgreSQL is installed. On Redhat/CentOS, run this command by substituting the package name with one that matches the version of PostgreSQL:

```
$ yum install postgresql93-plpython
```

On Mac OS X, check the documentation for your PostgreSQL installation method. For example, using Homebrew, the following command installs PostgreSQL with `plpython` support:

```
$ brew install postgresql --with-python
```

Once PostgreSQL has been set up with `plpython`, follow the instructions at https://github.com/madlib/madlib/wiki/Installation-Guide to install MADlib. The user account being used to install MADlib needs superuser privileges, which can be granted by running `ALTER ROLE ruser WITH SUPERUSER;` in PostgreSQL.

Now, return to R and connect to PostgreSQL using the `RPostgreSQL` package:

```
db.drv <- PostgreSQL()
db.conn <- dbConnect(db.drv, host = "hostname",
                port = 5432, dbname = "rdb",
                user = "ruser",
                password = "rpassword")
```

Say we want to mine our sales database for association rules. As you can remember from *Chapter 6, Simple Tweaks to Use Less RAM*, the `arules` package provides functions to mine for frequent itemsets and association rules. In order to use the `arules` package, the entire `trans_items` table would need to be extracted into R and converted into a `transactions` object. If the dataset is large, this might take a long time, or might not be possible at all.

Alternatively, we can mine the association rules in the database using MADlib functions. The data does not need to be copied out of the database at all, and all the computations can take place in the database as long as the database server or cluster has sufficient capacity.

Running the association rules mining algorithm is as simple as calling the `madlib.assoc_rules()` function in an SQL SELECT statement:

```
dbGetQuery(
    db.conn,
    "SELECT *
    FROM madlib.assoc_rules(
        0.001,           -- support
        0.01,            -- confidence
        'trans_id',      -- tid_col
        'item_id',       -- item_col
        'trans_items',   -- input_table
        'public',        -- output_schema
        TRUE             -- verbose
    );")
## INFO:   finished checking parameters
## CONTEXT:  PL/Python function "assoc_rules"
## INFO:   finished removing duplicates
## CONTEXT:  PL/Python function "assoc_rules"
## # Output truncated
## INFO:  6 Total association rules found. Time: 0.00557494163513
## CONTEXT:  PL/Python function "assoc_rules"
##   output_schema output_table total_rules     total_time
## 1        public  assoc_rules          6 00:01:21.860964
```

The preceding code includes comments that describe the arguments to `madlib.assoc_rules()`. Here, the algorithm is asked to search for association rules with a support of at least 0.001 and confidence of at least 0.01. The name of the input table and columns are specified, as well as the name of the schema in which you can store the results. In this case, the results will be stored in a table called `assoc_rules` in the `public` schema.

Every time the function is run, the `assoc_rules` table will be overwritten; so if you would like to keep a copy of the results, you will have to make a copy of the table.

Let's retrieve the results, that is, the association rules that meet the minimum support and confidence:

```
dbGetQuery(
    db.conn,
    'SELECT * FROM assoc_rules;')
##   ruleid    pre    post support confidence      lift conviction
## 1      1  {353}  {656}   1e-04 0.02272727 5.516328   1.019040
## 2      2  {656}  {353}   1e-04 0.02427184 5.516328   1.020366
## 3      3  {770}  {420}   1e-04 0.02444988 6.022137   1.020901
## 4      4  {420}  {770}   1e-04 0.02463054 6.022137   1.021059
## 5      5  {755}  {473}   1e-04 0.02469136 6.203859   1.021236
## 6      6  {473}  {755}   1e-04 0.02512563 6.203859   1.021619
```

The results indicate the items on the left- and right-hand sides of each association rule, along with the statistics for each rule such as the support, confidence, lift, and conviction.

Most of the other MADlib functions work in a similar way—data is supplied to a function in a database table, the function is called with the appropriate arguments, and the results are written to a new database table in the specified schema.

> Because Pivotal, Inc. developed both the `PivotalR` package and MADlib, it is natural that `PivotalR` provides interfaces to some MADlib functions such as linear models, ARIMA time series models and decision trees. It also provides useful functions to extract information such as regression coefficients from the MADlib output. Unfortunately, `PivotalR` does not provide wrappers to all the MADlib functions such as the `madlib.assoc_rules()` function used in the preceding code. For maximum flexibility in using the MADlib library, use SQL statements to call the MADlib functions.

In-database analytics libraries such as MADlib allow us to harness the power of advanced analytics in large databases and bring the results of the algorithms into R for further analysis and processing.

Using columnar databases for improved performance

Most relational databases use a row-based data storage architecture — the data is stored in the database row by row. Whenever the database performs a query, it retrieves the relevant rows for the query before processing the query. This architecture is well suited for business transactional uses, where complete records (that is, including all columns) are written, read, updated, or deleted, a few rows at a time. For most statistical or analytical use cases, however, many rows of data, often with only a few columns, need to be read. As a result, row-based databases are sometimes inefficient at analytical tasks because they read entire records at a time regardless of how many columns are actually needed for analysis. The following figure depicts how a row-based database might compute the sum of one column.

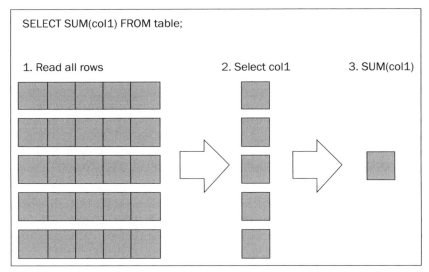

Computing the sum of one column in a row-based database

The increase in demand for data analysis platforms in recent years has led to the development of databases that use alternative storage architectures that are optimized for data analysis instead of business transactions. One such architecture is **columnar storage**. Columnar databases store data in columns instead of rows. This is very similar to R data frames where each column of a data frame is stored in a contiguous block of memory in the form of an R vector. When computing the sum of one column, a columnar database needs to read only one column of data, as shown in the following figure:

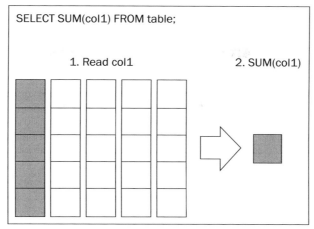

SELECT SUM(col1) FROM table;

1. Read col1   2. SUM(col1)

Computing the sum of one column in a columnar database

One example of a columnar database is MonetDB, which can be downloaded from
`https://www.monetdb.org/Downloads`. Follow the instructions there to install it.
After installation, take the following steps to initialize and start the database.

On Linux or Mac OS X, run the following commands in a terminal window:

```
# Create a new database farm
# (Replace the path with a location of your choice)
$ monetdbd create /path/to/mydbfarm
# Start the database server
$ monetdbd start /path/to/mydbfarm
# Create a new database within the farm
$ monetdb create rdb
# Release the new database from administration locks
$ monetdb release rdb
```

On Windows, initialize and start the server by going to **Start** | **Programs** |
MonetDB | **Start server**.

Because MonetDB is based on SQL, connecting to and working with MonetDB from
R is similar to working with PostgreSQL. We can either execute SQL statements
using the MonetDB.R CRAN package or use dplyr. For example, we can load the
same sales and transaction data into MonetDB using MonetDB.R:

```
library(MonetDB.R)
db.drv <- MonetDB.R()
db.conn <- dbConnect(db.drv, host = "hostname",
```

```
                    port = 50000, dbname = "rdb",
                    user = "monetdb",
                    password = "monetdb")
dbWriteTable(db.conn, "sales", sales)
dbWriteTable(db.conn, "trans_items", trans.items)
```

Now, let's benchmark the query performance for the same SQL queries used in the RPostgreSQL examples:

```
library(microbenchmark)
microbenchmark({
    res <- dbGetQuery(
        db.conn,
        'SELECT store_id, SUM(price) as total_sales
        FROM sales INNER JOIN trans_items USING (trans_id)
        GROUP BY store_id;')
}, times = 10)
## Unit: milliseconds
##       min       lq   median       uq      max neval
##  112.1666 113.0484 113.9021 114.4349 114.7049    10
microbenchmark({
    res <- dbGetQuery(
        db.conn,
        'SELECT cust_id, SUM(price) as spending
        FROM sales INNER JOIN trans_items USING (trans_id)
        GROUP BY cust_id
        ORDER BY spending DESC
        LIMIT 10;')
}, times = 10)
## Unit: milliseconds
##       min       lq   median       uq      max neval
##  114.2376 115.4617  116.515 117.1967 118.4736    10
```

Compared to PostgreSQL, MonetDB took 55 percent less time for both queries (as you can remember from before that the median times needed by PostgreSQL for the first and second queries were 251.1 and 260.1 milliseconds, respectively). Of course, this is not a comprehensive or rigorous comparison between row-based and columnar databases, but it gives an indication of the performance gains that can be achieved by selecting the right database architecture for the task at hand.

Using array databases for maximum scientific-computing performance

Columnar databases provide good query performance for datasets that resemble R data frames, for example, most data from business IT systems. These datasets are usually two dimensional and can contain heterogeneous data types. On the other hand, scientific data sometimes contain homogeneous data types but are multidimensional. An example of this is weather readings in different points in time and space. For such applications, a new type of database called the **array database** provides even better query and scientific computing performance. One example of this is SciDB, available for download at `http://www.scidb.org/`. SciDB provides a **massively parallel processing (MPP)** architecture that can perform queries in parallel on petabytes of array data. It supports in-database linear algebra, graph operations, linear models, correlations, and statistical tests. It also offers an R interface through the SciDB package that is available on CRAN.

To download and install SciDB, follow the instructions at `https://github.com/Paradigm4/deployment`. Then, install `shim` (`https://github.com/paradigm4/shim`) on the SciDB server, which is needed for R in order to communicate with SciDB. Finally, install the `scidb` package from CRAN.

Connect to the SciDB database using the `scidbconnect()` function:

```
library(scidb)
scidbconnect(host = "hostname", port = 8080)
```

We can then load some data into the database using `as.scidb()`:

```
A <- as.scidb(matrix(rnorm(1200), 40, 30), name = "A")
B <- as.scidb(matrix(rnorm(1200), 30, 40), name = "B")
```

`scidb` provides familiar R syntax to manipulate SciDB matrices and arrays:

```
# Matrix multiplication
A %*% B
# Transpose and addition / subtraction
A + t(B)
# Scalar operations
A * 1.5
```

We can even mix SciDB matrices/arrays with R matrices/arrays:

```
C <- matrix(rnorm(1200), 30, 40)
A %*% C
```

As with the other database packages, operations are not actually performed until the results are retrieved. In the case of `SciDB`, the `[]` operator causes the database to perform the computations and return the results:

```
# Filter only the positive elements of A, and materialize the
# results into R
(A > 0)[]
```

`SciDB` supports many other common array/matrix operations such as subsetting, comparison, filtering, apply, joining, aggregation, and sorting. It is a powerful tool for working with large, multidimensional numerical data.

Summary

In this chapter, we took a tour of various database systems and the R packages that allow us to interface with them, and saw how in-database querying and analysis can provide better performance than copying the data into R to do the same analysis. This is especially true for large datasets that cannot be easily processed in R; using a database that is tuned for querying and analysis can help to avoid performance issues in R. As technology improves, more and more advanced analysis and algorithms can be run in databases providing more options for R programmers who face the challenge of analyzing large datasets efficiently. These powerful data processing tools can complement R very nicely—they provide the computing muscle to analyze large datasets, while R provides easy interfaces for data manipulation and analysis. R can also help to bring together different threads of analyses, regardless of the tool used, to present a coherent and compelling picture of the data using tools such as data visualization.

In the next and final chapter, we will go to the frontiers of Big Data and take a look at how R can be used alongside Big Data tools to process extremely large datasets.

10
R and Big Data

We have come to the final chapter of this book where we will go to the very limits of large-scale data processing. The term *Big Data* has been used to describe the ever growing volume, velocity, and variety of data being generated on the Internet in connected devices and many other places. Many organizations now have massive datasets that measure in petabytes (one petabyte is 1,048,576 gigabytes), more than ever before. Processing and analyzing Big Data is extremely challenging for traditional data processing tools and database architectures.

In 2005, Doug Cutting and Mike Cafarella at Yahoo! developed Hadoop, based on earlier work by Google, to address these challenges. They set out to develop a new data platform to process, index, and query billions of web pages efficiently. With Hadoop, the work which would have previously required very expensive supercomputers can now be done on large clusters of inexpensive standard servers. As the volume of data grows, more servers can simply be added to a Hadoop cluster to increase the storage capacity and computing power. Since then, Hadoop and its ecosystem of tools has become one of the most popular suites of tools to collect, store, process and analyze large datasets. In this chapter, we will learn how to tap into the power of Hadoop from R.

This chapter covers the following topics:

- Understanding Hadoop
- Setting up Hadoop on Amazon Web Services
- Processing large datasets in batches using RHadoop

Understanding Hadoop

Before we learn how to use Hadoop (for more information refer to `http://hadoop.apache.org/`) and related tools in R, we need to understand the basics of Hadoop. For our purposes, it suffices to know that Hadoop comprises two key components: the **Hadoop Distributed File System (HDFS)** and the **MapReduce** framework to execute data processing tasks. Hadoop includes many other components for task scheduling, job management, and others, but we shall not concern ourselves with those in this book.

HDFS, as the name suggests, is a virtual filesystem that is distributed across a cluster of servers. HDFS stores files in blocks, with a default block size of 128 MB. For example, a 1 GB file is split into eight blocks of 128 MB, which are distributed to different servers in the cluster. Furthermore, to prevent data loss due to server failure, the blocks are replicated. By default, they are replicated three times — there are three copies of each block of data in the cluster, and each copy is stored on a different server. That way, even if a few servers in the cluster fail, the data is not lost and can be re-replicated to ensure high availability.

MapReduce is the framework to process the data stored in HDFS in a data parallel way. Notice how the distributed nature of data storage makes Hadoop a good fit for data parallel algorithms that we learned about in *Chapter 8, Multiplying Performance with Parallel Computing* — the chunks of data stored on each worker node are processed simultaneously in parallel, and then the results from each node are combined to produce the final results. MapReduce works very similarly to the data parallel algorithms in *Chapter 8, Multiplying Performance with Parallel Computing*, except that the data already resides in the worker nodes; it does not have to be distributed every time a task is run as was the case with a cluster of servers that run R. **Map** refers to the step of performing computations on the data in each worker node, or mapping data to their corresponding output. **Reduce** refers to the process of combining, or reducing the results of the worker nodes into the final results.

Data in MapReduce is represented as key-value pairs. Every MapReduce operation is essentially a transformation from one set of key-value pairs to another set of key-value pairs. A **mapper** might, for example, read a single customer record from a database and produce a key-value pair such as (`"Alice "`, `32`) that contains the name of a customer (`"Alice"`) as the key and the reward points she or he collected in a given week (`32`) as the corresponding value. After the map step, all the key-value pairs are sorted by the key, and the pairs with the same key are given to individual **reducers**. So, for example, there would be one reducer for all pairs with the key `"Alice"`, another reducer for the key `"Bob"`, and another for `"Charlie"`. A reducer takes all the key-value pairs it is given, performs computations on them, and returns the results as another key-value pair.

The reducers in our simple example could compute the mean of weekly reward points collected by all customers. The MapReduce system then collects the results of all the reducers as the final output, which could be something like [("Alice", 26.5), ("Bob", 42.3), ("Charlie", 35.6), ...].

While HDFS and MapReduce are the foundation of Hadoop, they are not suited for all data processing tasks. One key reason is that data stored in HDFS resides on the hard drives of the servers. Each time a MapReduce task is performed, the data has to be read from the disk, and the results of the computations are written back to the disk. Thus, HDFS and MapReduce perform reasonably well for sizeable batch processing tasks where the time to complete the computational tasks exceeds the overheads of reading/writing data and other overheads of running a Hadoop cluster.

Setting up Hadoop on Amazon Web Services

There are many ways to set up a Hadoop cluster. We can install Hadoop on a single server in pseudo-distributed mode to simulate a cluster, or on an actual cluster of servers, or virtual machines in fully distributed mode. There are also several distributions of Hadoop available from the vanilla open source version provided by the Apache Foundation to commercial distributions such as Cloudera, Hortonworks, and MapR. Covering all the different ways of setting up Hadoop is beyond the scope of this book. We instead provide instructions for one way to set up Hadoop and other relevant tools for the purpose of the examples in this chapter. If you are using an existing Hadoop cluster or setting up one in a different way, you might have to modify some of the steps.

Because Hadoop and its associated tools are mostly developed for Linux/Unix based operating systems, the code in this chapter will probably not work on Windows. If you are a Windows user, follow the instructions in this chapter to set up Hadoop, R, and the required packages on Amazon Web Services.

Amazon Web Services (AWS) has a service called **Elastic MapReduce (EMR)** that allows us to rent and run a Hadoop cluster on an hourly basis. Creating a Hadoop cluster is as simple as specifying the number of servers in the cluster, the size of each server, and the instructions to set up the required tools on each server. To set up an account with AWS, follow the instructions in *Preface*. Running the examples in this chapter on AWS will cost some money for as long as the EMR cluster is running. Check this link out http://aws.amazon.com/elasticmapreduce/pricing/ for the latest EMR prices.

We also need a script that sets up the required tools on each server. Save the following script as `emr-bootstrap.sh`. This scripts installs the R packages needed for this chapter, including `rhdfs`, `rmr2`, and `R.utils` on every server in the Hadoop cluster.

```bash
#!/bin/bash
# Set unix environment variables
cat << EOF >> $HADOOP_HOME/.bashrc
export HADOOP_CMD=$HADOOP_HOME/bin/hadoop
export HADOOP_STREAMING=$HADOOP_HOME/contrib/streaming/hadoop-
streaming.jar
EOF
. $HADOOP_HOME/.bashrc
# Fix hadoop tmp permission
sudo chmod 777 -R /mnt/var/lib/hadoop/tmp
# Install dependencies
sudo yum install -y libcurl-devel
# Install R packages
sudo -E R CMD javareconf
sudo -E R --no-save << EOF
install.packages("R.utils", repos="http://cran.rstudio.com")
EOF
# Install HadoopR dependencies
sudo -E R --no-save << EOF
install.packages(
    c("bitops", "caTools", "digest", "functional", "plyr", "Rcpp",
      "reshape2", "rJava", "RJSONIO", "stringr"),
    repos="http://cran.rstudio.com")
EOF
# Install rhdfs package
wget https://raw.githubusercontent.com/RevolutionAnalytics/rhdfs/
master/build/rhdfs_1.0.8.tar.gz
sudo -E R CMD INSTALL rhdfs_1.0.8.tar.gz
# Install rmr2 package
wget https://raw.githubusercontent.com/RevolutionAnalytics/rmr2/
master/build/rmr2_3.2.0.tar.gz
sudo -E R CMD INSTALL rmr2_3.2.0.tar.gz
```

Upload `emr-bootstrap.sh` into the AWS Simple Storage Service (S3) so that the EMR servers can pick it up during the first run. To do this:

1. Go to the AWS console, and click on **S3**.

2. Create a new bucket to store the script in by clicking on **Create Bucket**.

3. Click on the bucket that was just created and click on **Upload** to upload the script.

Next, follow these steps to create the Hadoop cluster:

1. Go to the AWS Console and click on **EMR**.

2. Click on **Create cluster**.

3. Under **Software Configuration**, select the Amazon Hadoop distribution (the examples in this chapter were tested with Amazon Machine Image (AMI) version 3.2.1).

4. Remove Hive and Pig from the applications list, as they are not needed.

5. Under **Hardware Configuration**, select the instance types for the Hadoop servers. The instance types for both the master and core nodes should have at least 15 GB of RAM, such as the m1.xlarge or m3.xlarge instance types. Enter the number of nodes you would like in the cluster. Given the default HDFS replication factor of three, there should be at least three core nodes. Task nodes are optional.

6. Under **Security and Access**, select the EC2 key pair to log in to the cluster with.

7. Under **Bootstrap Actions**, select **Custom action,** then click on **Configure and add**. In the dialog box that appears under **S3 location**, enter or browse for the S3 location where emr-bootstrap.sh was uploaded.

8. (Optional) Enable logging under **Cluster Configuration** to have all Hadoop logs automatically stored in the S3 bucket. To use this option, first create an S3 bucket to store the logs in, and enter the name of the bucket in the **Log folder S3 location** field. While optional, storing Hadoop logs is useful for tracing errors and debugging, which can be challenging without the logs, as an executed program gets spawned across multiple processes and computer nodes in Hadoop.

9. Click on **Create cluster** and wait a few minutes while the cluster is being set up.

Once the EMR cluster is ready, get the Master Public DNS from the cluster details page, and log in to the master server from the command line using your AWS EC2 security key (replace hadoop.pem with the name of your key):

```
$ ssh -i hadoop.pem root@master-public-dns
```

Once you are logged in, run R, which comes preinstalled with the EMR cluster:

```
$ R
```

Processing large datasets in batches using Hadoop

Batch processing is the most basic type of task that HDFS and MapReduce can perform. Similar to the data parallel algorithms in *Chapter 8, Multiplying Performance with Parallel Computing*, the master node sends a set of instructions to the worker nodes, which execute the instructions on the blocks of data stored on them. The results are then written to the disk in HDFS.

When an aggregate result is required, both the map and reduce steps are performed on the data. For example, in order to compute the mean of a distributed dataset, the mappers on the worker nodes first compute the sum and number of elements in each local chunk of data. The reducers then add up all these results to compute the global mean.

At other times, only the map step is performed when aggregation is not required. This is common in data transformation or cleaning operations where the data is simply being transformed form one format to another. One example of this is extracting email addresses from a set of documents. In this case, the results of the mappers on the worker nodes are stored as new datasets in HDFS, and reducers are not needed.

The R community has developed several packages to perform MapReduce tasks from R. One of these is the RHadoop family of packages developed by Revolution Analytics (for more information refer to https://github.com/RevolutionAnalytics/RHadoop). RHadoop includes the packages rhdfs, which provides functions to manipulate files and directories in HDFS, and rmr2, which exposes the functionality of MapReduce as R functions. These functions make it easy to use MapReduce without having to program with the Hadoop Java APIs. Instead, rmr2 runs a copy of R on every worker node, and the mappers and reducers are written as R functions to be applied on each chunk of data.

If you did not use the Hadoop setup instructions in the preceding section, follow the installation instructions for rhdfs and rmr2 at https://github.com/RevolutionAnalytics/RHadoop/wiki.

Uploading data to HDFS

The first thing to do for this is to get data into HDFS. For this chapter, we will use the Google Books Ngrams data (for more information refer to `http://storage.googleapis.com/books/ngrams/books/datasetsv2.html`). Here, n-grams are consecutive words that appear in the text where *n* represents the number of words in a phrase—a 1-gram is simply a word (for example, "Batman"), a 2-gram is two consecutive words (for example, "Darth Vader"), and a 6-gram is six consecutive words (for example, "Humpty Dumpty sat on a wall"). We will use the data of 1-grams for our examples.

 The dataset for this chapter is large enough to test the performance of Hadoop on a small cluster, but it is still relatively small compared to many other real-world datasets. Tools such as `ffdf` (*Chapter 7, Processing Large Datasets with Limited RAM*) can probably be used to process this dataset on a single machine. But when the data size gets much larger, Hadoop or other Big Data tools might be the only way to process the data.

The following code downloads the 1-grams data and uploads them into HDFS. Google provides the data in separate files, with one file for each letter of the alphabet containing the words that start with that letter. In this code, `hdfs.init()` first initializes the connection to HDFS. Then, `hdfs.mkdir()` creates the directory `/ngrams/data` in HDFS where the data will be stored. The code in the `for` loop downloads each file, decompresses it, and uploads it to HDFS using `hdfs.put()`:

```
library(rhdfs)
library(R.utils)
hdfs.init()
hdfs.mkdir("/ngrams/data")
files <- paste0("googlebooks-eng-all-1gram-20120701-", letters)
for (f in files) {
    gzfile <- paste0(f, ".gz")
    url <- paste0("http://storage.googleapis.com/",
                  "books/ngrams/books/",
                  gzfile)
    download.file(url, destfile = gzfile)
    gunzip(gzfile)
    hdfs.put(f, paste0("/ngrams/data/", f))
    file.remove(f)
}
```

We can check that all the files have been uploaded successfully into HDFS:

```
hdfs.ls("/ngrams/data")
## permission  owner   group        size        modtime
## 1  -rw-r--r--  hadoop supergroup 1801526075 2014-10-05 09:59
## 2  -rw-r--r--  hadoop supergroup 1268392934 2014-10-05 10:00
## 3  -rw-r--r--  hadoop supergroup 2090710388 2014-10-05 10:01
## 4  -rw-r--r--  hadoop supergroup 1252213884 2014-10-05 10:01
## 5  -rw-r--r--  hadoop supergroup 1085415448 2014-10-05 10:02
## file
## 1  /ngrams/data/googlebooks-eng-all-1gram-20120701-a
## 2  /ngrams/data/googlebooks-eng-all-1gram-20120701-b
## 3  /ngrams/data/googlebooks-eng-all-1gram-20120701-c
## 4  /ngrams/data/googlebooks-eng-all-1gram-20120701-d
## 5  /ngrams/data/googlebooks-eng-all-1gram-20120701-e
## $ hdfs dfs -du -h /ngrams
# Output truncated
```

Analyzing HDFS data with RHadoop

Now that the data is loaded into HDFS, we can use MapReduce to analyze the data. Say we want to compare the popularity of Batman versus Superman since the 1950s. The Google Ngrams data might provide some insight into that.

Each line of the Ngrams data is a tab-seperated list of values, starting with the Ngram, followed by the year, number of occurrences of that Ngram, and number of books that the Ngram appeared in. For example, the following command line indicates that in 1978, the word "mountain" appeared 1,435,642 times in 1,453 books in the Google Books library.

```
mountain    1978    1435642    1453
```

To compare the popularity of Batman and Superman, we need to find the lines of code that represent these two words from 1950 onwards and collate the occurrence values.

Since the data consists of tab-separated text files, we need to specify the input format so that the `rmr2` functions know how to read the files. This can be done using the `make.input.format()` function:

```
library(rmr2)
input.format <- make.input.format(
    format = "csv", sep = "\t",
    col.names = c("ngram", "year", "occurrences", "books"),
    colClasses = c("character", "integer", "integer", "integer"))
```

For delimited text files such as comma-separated values or tab-separated values, `make.input.format()` accepts most of the same arguments as `read.table()`. In fact, `rmr2` uses `read.table()` to read each chunk of data into a data frame.

Besides delimited text files, `rmr2` can also read/write data as raw text (`format = "text"`), JSON (`"json"`), R's internal data serialization format (`"native"`), Hadoop SequenceFiles (`"sequence.typedbytes"`), HBase tables (`"hbase"`), and Hive or Pig (`"pig.hive"`). See the package documentation for the arguments associated with these data types.

The map step of our analysis involves filtering each line of data to find the relevant records. We will define a `mapper` function, as shown in the following code, that accepts a set of keys and a set of values as arguments. Since the Ngrams data does not contain keys, the `keys` argument is NULL. The argument `values` is a data frame that contains a chunk of data. The mapper function looks for rows of the data frame that contain the words we are interested in, for the year 1950 or later. If any relevant rows are found, the `keyval()` function is called to return key-value pairs that will be passed to the reduce function. In this case, the keys are the words and the values are the corresponding years and occurrence counts:

```
mapper <- function(keys, values) {
    values$ngram <- tolower(values$ngram)
    superheroes <- values$ngram %in% c("batman", "superman") &
        values$year >= 1950L
    if (any(superheroes)) {
        keyval(values$ngram[superheroes],
                values[superheroes, c("year", "occurrences")])
    }
}
```

If you are familiar with MapReduce, you might have noticed that `rmr2` allows the mapper to accept and emit key-value pairs as lists and data frames that represent a whole chunk of data instead of one record at a time, as is the case with classical MapReduce. This can help with R's performance; vectorized R operations can be used to process the whole chunk of data.

The next step occurs behind the scenes, where MapReduce collects all the data emitted by the mappers and groups them by key. In this example, it will find two groups that correspond to the `"batman"` and `"superman"` keys. MapReduce then calls the reducer function to process one group of data at a time.

The job of the reducer, given the data for a particular superhero, is to sum the number of occurrences of this superhero's name by year, using `tapply()`. This is required because the words in the Ngrams dataset are case sensitive. So, for example, we need to add up the number of times that "Batman", "batman", and "BATMAN" appear in each year. The reducer then returns the superhero's name as the key, and a data frame that contains the total number of occurrences by year as the value. The code for the reducer is shown here:

```
reducer <- function(key, values) {
    val <- tapply(values$occurrences, values$year, sum)
    val <- data.frame(year = as.integer(names(val)),
                      occurrences = val)
    keyval(key, val)
}
```

Now that we have defined our mapper and reducer functions, we can execute the MapReduce job using `mapreduce()`. We will call this function, specify the input directory and data format, the output directory where the results are to be written, and the mapper and reducer functions.

```
job <- mapreduce(input = "/ngrams/data",
                 input.format = input.format,
                 output = "/ngrams/batmanVsuperman",
                 map = mapper, reduce = reducer)
```

When this MapReduce job executes, the resultant key-value pairs are written to HDFS in the /ngrams/batmanVsuperman folder. We can use `from.dfs()` to retrieve the results from HDFS into R objects. This function returns a list with two components: `key` and `value`. In this case, `key` is a character vector that specifies the superhero's name for each row of data, and `val` is a data frame that contains the corresponding years and occurrence counts.

```
results <- from.dfs(job)
batman <- results$val[results$key == "batman", ]
head(batman)
##      year occurrences
## 1950 1950         153
## 1951 1951         105
## 1952 1952         173
## 1953 1953         133
```

```
## 1954 1954            359
## 1955 1955            150
superman <- results$val[results$key == "superman", ]
head(superman)
##        year occurrences
## 1950 1950          1270
## 1951 1951          1130
## 1952 1952          1122
## 1953 1953           917
## 1954 1954          1222
## 1955 1955          1087
```

Let's plot the results in order to compare how popular these two superheroes have been over the years:

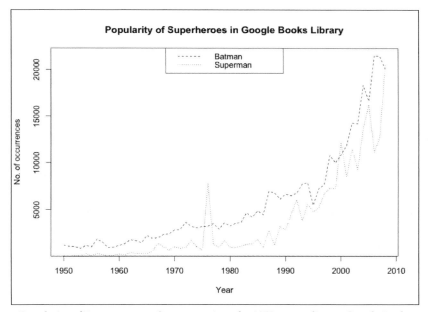

Popularity of Batman versus Superman since the 1950s, according to Google Books

While both the superheroes popularity steadily increased over the years, there is an interesting spike in the number of times Superman was mentioned in books in the 1970s. This could be due to the release of the multi Academy Award-winning film, *Superman* starring Christopher Reeve in 1978. However, this surge in popularity was short-lived.

The time it takes to complete the MapReduce algorithm depends on the size of the data, the complexity of the task, and the number of nodes in the cluster. We tested this example using the `m1.xlarge` AWS servers, which have 4 CPUs and 15 GB of RAM each, with cluster sizes ranging from 4 to 32 core nodes (in EMR terminology, these are nodes that store data and process them). The following figure shows how the execution time decreases as more nodes are added to the cluster:

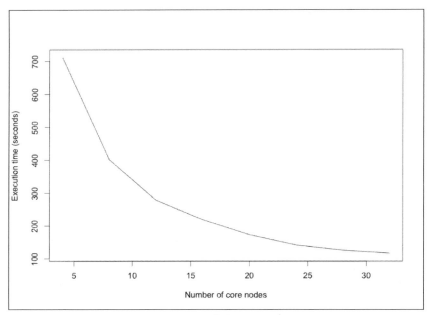

Execution time as cluster size increases

Because `rmr2` starts an instance of R on each Hadoop node to process the data, the efficiency of the MapReduce task depends on that of the R code for the mapper and reducer functions. Many of the techniques in this book to improve the performance of serial R programs can be applied when you design the mapper and reducer functions too. Furthermore, every MapReduce job incurs overheads of starting a new job, reading data from the disk, and coordinating the execution of the job across the cluster. Where possible, combining individual tasks into larger MapReduce tasks that can be executed at one go will help to improve the overall performance by reducing these overheads.

Once you are done using the Hadoop cluster, remember to terminate the cluster from the AWS EMR console to prevent unexpected charges.

Other Hadoop packages for R

While the scope of this book allows us to cover only a few R packages that interface with Hadoop, the community has developed many more packages to bring the power of Hadoop to R. Here are a few more packages that can be useful:

Besides `rhdfs` and `rmr2`, RHadoop also provides other packages:

- `plyrmr`: It provides functionality similar to `plyr` on MapReduce
- `rhbase`: It provides functions to work with HBase data
- `ravro`: It provides reading/writing of data in the Avro format

Another family of packages called `RHIPE` (for more information refer to `http://www.datadr.org/`) provides similar MapReduce capabilities with a slightly different syntax:

- `RHIPE`: This package provides the core HDFS and MapReduce functionality
- `datadr`: It provides data manipulation capabilities similar to `plyr`/`dplyr`
- `Trelliscope`: It provides visualization of large datasets in HDFS

At the time of writing, `RHIPE` does not support YARN or MapReduce 2.0. An older version of Hadoop is required to use the `RHIPE` packages until this is fixed.

Another package, `Segue` (for more information refer to `https://code.google.com/p/segue/`) takes a different approach. It does not provide full MapReduce capabilities. Rather, it treats Amazon's EMR as an additional computational resource for computationally heavy R tasks. This is similar to cluster computing in *Chapter 8, Multiplying Performance with Parallel Computing*, but using EMR as the computational cluster. The `Segue` package provides the `emrlapply()` function that performs a parallel `lapply` operation on an EMR cluster; this is analogous to `mclapply()` from the `parallel` package.

Summary

In this chapter, we learned how to set up a Hadoop cluster on Amazon Elastic MapReduce, and how to use the RHadoop family of packages in order to analyze data in HDFS using MapReduce. We saw how the performance of the MapReduce task improves dramatically as more servers are added to the Hadoop cluster, but the performance eventually reaches a limit due to Amdahl's law (*Chapter 8, Multiplying Performance with Parallel Computing*).

Hadoop and its ecosystem of tools is rapidly evolving. Other tools are being actively developed to make Hadoop perform even better. For example, Apache Spark (`http://spark.apache.org/`) provides Resilient Distributed Datasets (RDDs) that store data in memory across a Hadoop cluster. This allows data to be read from HDFS once and to be used many times in order to dramatically improve the performance of interactive tasks like data exploration and iterative algorithms like gradient descent or k-means clustering. Another example is Apache Storm (`http://storm.incubator.apache.org/`) that allows you to process real-time data streams. Because these tools and their associated R interfaces are being actively developed, they will likely change by the time you read this book, so we have decided not to include them here. But they are worth looking into if you have specific needs like in-memory analytics or real-time data processing.

We have come to the end of the book. It has been an exhilarating journey looking at a whole spectrum of techniques to improve the performance of R programs, from optimizing memory utilization and computational speed to multiplying computational power with parallel programming and cluster computing. What we have covered here is only the basics; there is much more to learn about writing more efficient R code. There are other resources that dive into specific topics in far greater detail than we can here. Package documentation is always useful to read, though sometimes cryptic; sometimes, the only way to find out what works is to try. Of course, there is the great community of R users in online forums, mailing lists and other places, who are always eager to help with answers and tips.

We hope that you have enjoyed this book and learned from it as much as we have writing it. Thank you for joining us in this journey, and we wish you the very best in exploring the world of R high-performance computing.

Index

socket-based cluster 108
space complexity 15
sparse matrices
  using 89, 90
SQL
  R expressions, converting 127
  used, for data preprocessing in relational
    database 122-126
statically typed language 54
statistical algorithm
  executing 132-135
statistical modeling
  with gputools 68-71
symmetric matrices
  using 90
system.time() function, output elements
  elapsed time 21
  system time 20
  user time 20
system-wide resource utilization measure
  monitoring 31

T

task parallel algorithms
  implementing 109
  multiple tasks, executing 111, 112
  same task, executing 109-111
task parallelism
  about 106
  versus data parallelism 102-106

tasks
  executing, in parallel on cluster of
    computers 113-115
time complexity
  about 15
  demonstrating 17
  example 15, 16
transient storage allocation 63
Trelliscope package 153

U

user-controlled memory
  about 63
  type* Calloc(size_t n, type) function 63
  type* Realloc(any *p, size_t n, type)
    function 63
  void Free(any *p) function 63

V

vectorization 38, 39

X

Xcode Command Line Tools
  installing 54
  URL, for downloading 54

Thank you for buying
R High Performance Programming

About Packt Publishing

Packt, pronounced 'packed', published its first book, *Mastering phpMyAdmin for Effective MySQL Management*, in April 2004, and subsequently continued to specialize in publishing highly focused books on specific technologies and solutions.

Our books and publications share the experiences of your fellow IT professionals in adapting and customizing today's systems, applications, and frameworks. Our solution-based books give you the knowledge and power to customize the software and technologies you're using to get the job done. Packt books are more specific and less general than the IT books you have seen in the past. Our unique business model allows us to bring you more focused information, giving you more of what you need to know, and less of what you don't.

Packt is a modern yet unique publishing company that focuses on producing quality, cutting-edge books for communities of developers, administrators, and newbies alike. For more information, please visit our website at www.packtpub.com.

About Packt Open Source

In 2010, Packt launched two new brands, Packt Open Source and Packt Enterprise, in order to continue its focus on specialization. This book is part of the Packt Open Source brand, home to books published on software built around open source licenses, and offering information to anybody from advanced developers to budding web designers. The Open Source brand also runs Packt's Open Source Royalty Scheme, by which Packt gives a royalty to each open source project about whose software a book is sold.

Writing for Packt

We welcome all inquiries from people who are interested in authoring. Book proposals should be sent to author@packtpub.com. If your book idea is still at an early stage and you would like to discuss it first before writing a formal book proposal, then please contact us; one of our commissioning editors will get in touch with you.

We're not just looking for published authors; if you have strong technical skills but no writing experience, our experienced editors can help you develop a writing career, or simply get some additional reward for your expertise.

R Object-Oriented Programming

ISBN: 978-1-78398-668-2   Paperback: 190 pages

A practical guide to help you learn and understand the programming techniques necessary to exploit the full power of R

1. Learn and understand the programming techniques necessary to solve specific problems and speed up development processes for statistical models and applications.

2. Explore the fundamentals of building objects and how they program individual aspects of larger data designs.

3. Step-by-step guide to understand how OOP can be applied to application and data models within R.

Instant R Starter

ISBN: 978-1-78216-350-3   Paperback: 54 pages

Jump into the R programming language and go beyond "Hello World!"

1. Learn something new in an Instant! A short, fast, focused guide delivering immediate results.

2. Basic concepts of the R language.

3. Discover tips and tricks for working with R.

4. Learn manipulation of R objects to easily customize your code.

Please check **www.PacktPub.com** for information on our titles

R for Data Science

ISBN: 978-1-78439-086-0   Paperback: 364 pages

Learn and explore the fundamentals of data science with R

1. Familiarize yourself with R programming packages and learn how to utilize them effectively.

2. Learn how to detect different types of data mining sequences.

3. A step-by-step guide to understanding R scripts and the ramifications of your changes.

R Graph Essentials [Video]

ISBN: 978-1-78216-546-0   Duration: 01:57 hrs

A visual and practical approach to learning how to create statistical graphs using R

1. Learn the basics of R graphs and how to make them.

2. Customize your graphs according to your specific needs without using overcomplicated techniques/packages.

3. Step-by-step instructions to create a wide range of professional-looking graphs.

Please check **www.PacktPub.com** for information on our titles

Printed in Great Britain
by Amazon.co.uk, Ltd.,
Marston Gate.